Big
Bone Lick

——— ❧ ———

Big
Bone Lick

———— ∾ ————

The Cradle of American Paleontology

Stanley Hedeen

Foreword by John Mack Faragher

THE UNIVERSITY PRESS OF KENTUCKY

Frontispiece: Museum exhibit depicting Big Bone Lick at the end of the Ice Age.
(Cincinnati Museum Center)

Editorial and Sales Offices: The University Press of Kentucky
663 South Limestone Street, Lexington, Kentucky 40508-4008
www.kentuckypress.com

12 11 10 09 08   5 4 3 2 1

Library of Congress Cataloging-in-Publication Data
Hedeen, Stanley.
    Big Bone lick : the cradle of American paleontology / Stanley Hedeen ;
foreword by John Mack Faragher.
        p.   cm.
    Includes bibliographical references and index.
    ISBN 978-0-8131-2485-8 (hardcover : alk. paper)
    1. Paleontology—Kentucky—Big Bone. 2. Mammoths—Kentucky—Big Bone.
3. Mastodons—Kentucky—Big Bone. 4. Mammals, Fossil—Kentucky—Big
Bone. 5. Fossils—Kentucky—Big Bone. 6. Big Bone (Ky.)--History. I. Title.
    QE705.U6H43 2008
    560.9769'363—dc22
                                                        2007040474

This book is printed on acid-free recycled paper meeting
the requirements of the American National Standard
for Permanence in Paper for Printed Library Materials.

Manufactured in the United States of America.

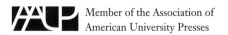

Member of the Association of
American University Presses

To Glenn Storrs,
Withrow Farny Curator of Vertebrate Paleontology,
Cincinnati Museum Center

Contents

Illustrations

Figures

Illustrations

Foreword

In 1784, Delaware schoolmaster John Filson published *The Discovery, Settlement, and Present State of Kentucke*, a tract promoting the trans-Appalachian West as the new "land of promise, flowing with milk and honey," and introducing readers to "The Adventures of Col. Daniel Boon." As a result, both Kentucky and Boone were soon famous—Kentucky as the first of many western American promised lands, and Boone as the archetypal man who led the way to them.

Filson offered something for everyone, packing his pages with descriptions of the many strange and curious things to be seen in the new West. None proved more interesting than the fossilized remains found at Big Bone Lick, a salt spring in what is now Boone County, near the Ohio River. Filson had visited the site himself soon after his arrival in Kentucky. The fossils he saw there were awesome: huge femur and rib bones, great ivory tusks, jawbones wider than the span of a man's arms, molars the size of pumpkins. These remains, Filson told his readers, exceeded "the size of any species of animals now in America." Specimens had already been collected and sent to Paris, London, and Philadelphia, where they "excited the amazement of the ignorant, and attracted the attention of the philosopher." They posed difficult questions. To what animal did they belong? Natives told "marvelous stories" about great beasts, but how could men of science trust such legends? The bones bore a resemblance to those of the elephant, but elephants were native to "the torrid zone" and could not possibly survive the frigid North American winters. Some authorities, Filson reported, argued that they were the remains of "a quadruped now unknown, and whose race is probably extinct," perhaps by the hand of man. "Can then so great a link have perished from the chain of nature?" It was all very perplexing. "These are difficulties," Filson concluded, "sufficient to stagger credulity itself."

Stanley Hedeen's delightful history recounts the fascinating story of the Big Bone Lick fossils. The tale moves far from Kentucky and includes a remarkable cast of characters. The site was well known to the native peoples of the Ohio Valley. Europeans first saw it in 1739, and soon specimens were being sent east and across the Atlantic. A number of Big Bone Lick fossils were deposited in the collections of the American Philosophical Society in Philadelphia; others resided in the Cabinet du Roi, the French king's collection of curiosities in Paris. Bones and teeth sent to London sparked debates before the Royal Society. The fossils even found their way into the Tammany Society's museum in New York City. Leading Americans such as Benjamin Franklin, George Washington, and Thomas Jefferson avidly sought specimens of their own.

The lust for these bones was, in part, simply a desire to see and touch something so spectacular. But as Filson's account suggests, there was also considerable controversy over the interpretation of the fossils. The Shawnee believed that they were the remains of man-eating monsters destroyed by a benevolent God to protect the Indian people. A noted British anatomist and physician to the queen agreed that they were the bones of a vanished species. "As men," he wrote, "we cannot but thank Heaven that its whole generation is probably extinct." But others, committed to a belief in the perfection of God's creation, found it hard to accept the notion of extinction. Thomas Jefferson thought that the very concept violated the inherent balance of nature, and he pondered the problem for many years. In the last months of his presidency, Jefferson commissioned William Clark, lately returned from his transcontinental exploration with Meriwether Lewis, to excavate and ship a large sampling of Big Bone Lick fossils to Washington. Hedeen's description of Jefferson laying out the bones in the East Room of the White House is only one of the many arresting images in this remarkable history.

Eventually, people made sense of the findings. Hedeen, himself a biologist, gives us the science as well as the history. His narrative strategy is simple but effective, letting the characters speak in their own voices, encouraging us to listen carefully to what the people of the past had to say. It makes for great reading.

John Mack Faragher
Arthur Unobskey Professor of American History
Yale University

Acknowledgments

I would like to thank Linda Lotz, Richard Davis, Greg Mc Donald, and Paul Semonin for their many suggestions for improving this book. A great deal of gratitude goes to Sidnie Reed for arranging numerous loans of library materials, and to John Mack Faragher for writing the foreword. Credit is also given to Greg Rust, Joe Higgins, and Kathy Hedeen for their assistance with the illustrations. Finally, special appreciation is extended to the professional and courteous staff of the University Press of Kentucky, especially Laura Sutton, Joyce Harrison, Ann Malcolm, Ila McEntire, and Will McKay.

Introduction

As no other place hitherto discovered in the Union has afforded such quantities of huge animal remains, . . . the
tomb of the mammoths will certainly reward the traveler
of taste and science.
—Daniel Drake, 1815

Big Bone Lick, "the tomb of the mammoths," became a Kentucky state park in 1960. Although not as well known as the
state's Mammoth Cave National Park, the salt lick is an equally
important geologic, biologic, and historic location. Most nota-
bly, the uncovering of the Lick's fossil bones called attention to
the fact that certain animals had vanished from the planet.

Several American Indian nations knew of Big Bone Lick
prior to its "discovery" by a French military party in 1739. Skeletal specimens taken from the site by the French commander
were placed in the king's natural history collection in Paris,
where they were studied by celebrated naturalists Georges-
Louis Leclerc de Buffon and Georges Cuvier. Kentucky frontier notables such as Daniel Boone, Mary Ingles, and George
Rogers Clark viewed the large bones at the Lick during the latter half of the eighteenth century. Visitors gathered fossils from
the location and provided them to Benjamin Franklin, George
Washington, and other prominent individuals. Captain Wil-

liam Henry Harrison, the future U.S. president, collected several barrels of fossils from the site.

Meriwether Lewis took bones from the Lick in the year prior to the 1804–1806 Lewis and Clark expedition, and his partner, William Clark, gathered hundreds of specimens in the year following the excursion. President Thomas Jefferson sponsored the activities of Lewis and Clark at the Lick, so some of the site's bones ended up at Jefferson's Monticello home. British scientist Charles Lyell, the "father of geology," made a pilgrimage to the famous Lick in 1842. Parties of university paleontologists amassed fossil troves for Harvard in the 1860s and Nebraska in the 1960s, and other collectors unearthed pieces for city, state, and national museums. A large number of American and foreign institutions house the thousands of fossil specimens that have been recovered from Big Bone Lick.

The purpose of this book is to present the remarkable story of the birthplace of American paleontology. The volume begins with an overview of the Lick's geology and its past human use as a source of salt and supposedly healthful mineral waters. The major portion of the text details the numerous discoveries of animal skeletal pieces, many of which were initially misidentified or misrepresented. The specimens collected from the Lick have been well characterized as the fossils "of which fame had said so much, the learned risked so many conjectures, and every body knew so little."[1] Finally, the last chapter examines the possible reasons for the disappearance of the site's extinct species and concludes with a description of how the salt lick's suspected source of brine might help prevent a future extinction event.

This is the second book bearing the title *Big Bone Lick*. The first text, a 1936 monograph by Willard Rouse Jillson, was sponsored by the Big Bone Lick Association. The present incarnation of the association is the Friends of Big Bone, a nonprofit group committed to providing education and conducting research at the Lick. Interested readers can contact the organization through its Web site or through the office at Big Bone Lick State Park.

Chapter 1

Geologic Setting

The most basic principle of geology is the Principle of Change. Given enough time, all things change. Thus also Big Bone.

—R. A. Davis, 1981

The eminent English geologist Charles Lyell visited the Cincinnati area in 1842 to collect two groups of fossils: mammal bones from Big Bone Lick, and marine shells from the bedrock of the region. Half a century earlier, upon discovering that the area's bedrock debris was "full of petrifactions of seashells," French naturalist André Michaux had concluded that the bones at the Lick were probably the remains of oceanic animals. Most early visitors to the Lick, however, correctly identified the site's bones as those of mammals that had lived on land sometime after the sea's disappearance from the Cincinnati region.[1]

Geologists today employ fission-track analysis, electron spin resonance, radiometric dating, and other techniques to estimate age. These methods have established that the Cincinnati area's marine invertebrate fossils are approximately 450 million years old, while the terrestrial mammal fossils at the Lick are less than 20,000 years old. Investigators have not yet determined the period when the Cincinnati area rose above sea level, but they have constructed a scenario of the region's emergence and its subsequent geologic history.[2]

1

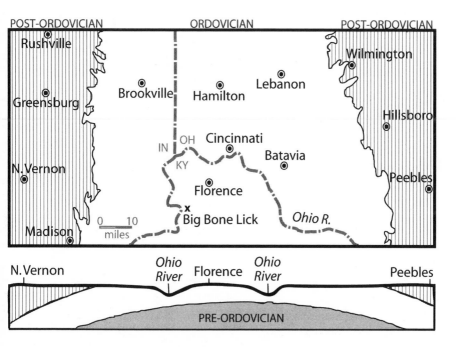

Figure 1. Relationship between surface bedrock (top map) and the Cincinnati Arch (bottom cross section). (Adapted from Kenneth E. Caster, Elizabeth A. Dalve, and John K. Pope, *Elementary Guide to the Fossils and Strata of the Ordovician in the Vicinity of Cincinnati, Ohio* [1961], 11)

The region's exposed fossiliferous strata started out about 450 million years ago as layers of bottom sediment in an ocean of the Ordovician period. Below the surface bedrock are sedimentary rock layers that were deposited earlier in oceans and tidal flats. One of these marine layers, possibly the pre-Ordovician Mount Simon Sandstone or the Ordovician St. Peter Sandstone, is the likely source of the sulfurous brine that flows from the salt springs at Big Bone Lick.[3]

Following the Ordovician period, oceans continued to cover the area for untold millions of years. The region eventually emerged above sea level when the portion of the continental plate below the Cincinnati area bulged upward. Today, the re-

Figure 2. Preglacial drainage of the Cincinnati region approximately 2 million years ago. (Adapted from James T. Teller, "Preglacial [Teays] and Early Glacial Drainage in the Cincinnati Area, Ohio, Kentucky, and Indiana," *Geological Society of America Bulletin* 84 [1973]: 3679, and Frank R. Ettensohn, "The Pre-Illinoian Lake Clays of the Cincinnati Region," *Ohio Journal of Science* 74 [1974]: 215)

gion still rests on the crest of the uplift, known as the Cincinnati Arch (figure 1). Erosion has removed the marine sediments that were deposited in the area after the Ordovician period.[4]

About 2 million years ago, just prior to the Pleistocene epoch, or the Ice Age, the Cincinnati area had a rolling to flat surface that was drained by low-gradient streams (figure 2). Modern evidence of the courses of these preglacial waterways is provided by stream sediments located just below the surface of today's uplands, as well as by paleochannels etched into the uplands. Investigators have found that the area's major preglacial streams flowed north, perhaps following underlying fault lines. Because streams seek the path of least resistance, they follow zones of weakness created by fractures in the earth's crust.[5]

Stream deposits from the preglacial Old Kentucky River are situated on the uplands near Big Bone Lick. In addition, a possible paleochannel of the preglacial Old Eagle Creek is found on these uplands, indicating that the Lick may be located near the site of the Old Eagle Creek's mouth on the Old Kentucky River. The occurrence of a preglacial stream channel in the vicinity of the Lick may be due to the subsurface fractures in the area. These fractures, which extend downward into the underlying sedimentary rock layers, serve as conduits for the sulfurous brine that surfaces in the Lick's springs.[6]

From the vicinity of the Lick, the Old Kentucky River continued northward, absorbing the Old Licking River as well as smaller streams. Some geologists theorize that the Old Kentucky River ran north all the way to the Erie Basin lowland. Others believe that the river emptied into a large east-west stream (the Teays River) that flowed across central Ohio, Indiana, and Illinois to drain into the Mississippi River in the vicinity of St. Louis.[7]

At least three Ice Age glaciers visited the Ohio River Valley: the pre-Illinoian, the Illinoian, and the Wisconsinan. Between 1 million and 2 million years ago, the southward advance of the pre-Illinoian glacier blocked the channel of the north-flowing Old Kentucky River. The same continental ice sheet also blocked the channels of other north-flowing streams located between the Cincinnati area and the Appalachian Highlands to the east. The glacial ice acted as a dam, causing lakes to form in the stream valleys. As each lake filled, it overflowed into the next lake, which subsequently overflowed into the next one, and so

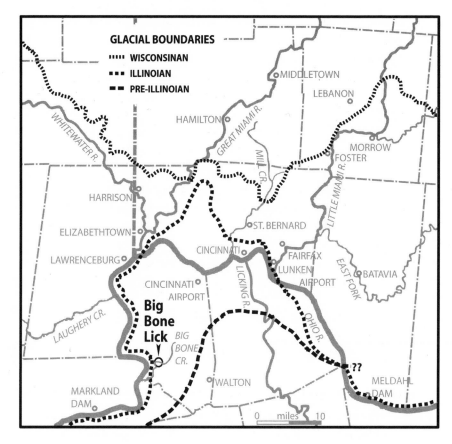

Figure 3. Glacial limits in the Cincinnati region. (Adapted from Louis L. Ray, "Geomorphology and Quaternary Geology of the Glaciated Ohio River Valley—A Reconnaissance Study," *U.S. Geological Survey Professional Paper 826* [1974], plate 1)

on, until the Ohio River drainage system to the west was formed along the margin of the ice sheet.[8]

When the pre-Illinoian ice sheet pushed into northern Kentucky, the glacier blanketed the site of Big Bone Lick, choked the northern portion of the Old Eagle Creek channel, and diverted the Ohio River southward around the edge of the ice.

The boundary of the ice sheet was located several miles to the south and east of the Lick at the time of the glacier's maximum advance (figure 3). Following the retreat of the glacier, the Ohio River cut its present valley near the Lick, and Eagle Creek established its current channel about ten miles southwest of the Lick.[9]

The pre-Illinoian glacial age was followed by an interglacial span of several hundred thousand years. During this interglacial age, the Big Bone Creek drainage system formed in the northern Kentucky region that had been drained by the preglacial Old Eagle Creek. Big Bone Lick is located along the valley floor of Big Bone Creek, about three miles from the stream's mouth on the Ohio River.

Approximately a quarter million years ago, the Cincinnati region was again visited by a continental ice sheet. This next-to-last glacier to reach the region is called the Illinoian because the first evidence of its existence was found in Illinois. Unlike the pre-Illinoian glacier, the Illinoian either did not cover Big Bone Lick or did not leave lasting indications of any landscape modifications at the site. The nearest glacial debris deposited by the Illinoian ice sheet is located about half a mile northwest of the Lick.[10]

The Illinoian glaciation gave way to a warmer interglacial period that lasted until the advent of the Wisconsinan glacial age. The Wisconsinan glacier, the last North American ice sheet, pushed into the Cincinnati region approximately 70,000 years ago and began its retreat about 19,500 years ago. This glacier stopped well short of Big Bone Lick—its nearest lobe stalled approximately thirty miles north of the site. Nevertheless, outwash materials from the Wisconsinan glacier had a large influence on the Lick's present topography.[11]

Wisconsinan glacier meltwater and debris poured into the Ohio River through streams located from New York to Indiana. At Big Bone Creek and other Ohio River tributaries, glacial sand and gravel moving down the Ohio River occasionally plugged the mouths of the tributary valleys. Each dam of glacial debris would impound the tributary and cause the erosion sediments from the tributary's watershed to settle to the bottom of the ponded stream.

Glacial debris dams have not formed at the mouth of Big Bone Creek valley since the end of the Ice Age 10,000 years ago. Consequently, at the Lick, there has been no recent major deposition of impoundment sediments derived from the Big Bone Creek watershed. However, erosion silt carried by the Ohio River continues to be deposited at the Lick during backwater floods. Sediment coring at the Lick has revealed that up to thirty-two feet of fill presently rests above the bedrock on the valley bottom.[12]

Following each major sedimentation event, Big Bone Creek renewed its pre-event channel or carved an alternative course through the Lick. The creek's movements back and forth across the valley floor have carried away or repositioned many of the silt deposits. The springs at Big Bone Lick push upward through the valley fill to reach the surface of the Lick, where they release their saline waters to flow into Big Bone Creek. The brine bubbling forth at the site has long attracted both animals and people to the Lick.[13]

Chapter 2

—— ❧ ——

Source of Salt and Health

I am satisfied that for retirement and recuperation this spot with its beautiful scenery, delightful atmosphere and El Doradoic waters is unexcelled by any on the American continent.

—S. E. J., 1876

Common salt (sodium chloride), an essential mineral for both animals and people, is found in the spring waters of Big Bone Lick. A typical adult human should maintain about 250 grams of salt in the body, enough to fill three to four average saltshakers. If a person does not take in enough salt to replace the amount lost through bodily functions, the body will increase its secretion of water in an attempt to maintain the salt concentration at a vital level. Over time, a salt-poor diet can cause the desiccation and eventual death of a person.[1]

Animal flesh is an excellent source of salt, allowing hunting-gathering humans with meat-based diets to forgo additional salt. People engaged in agriculture, in contrast, are required to supplement their plant-heavy diets with salt in a free form. Brine from saline springs has long been a major source of dietary salt for North Americans, starting with the agricultural Indian cultures. Their earliest method of obtaining salt from brine was the open-pan procedure, a technique used in many parts of the world since the beginning of recorded history. Brine was placed in ceramic or metal pans and heated by fire, leading to evaporation and the formation of salt crystals. The brine was continually replenished as evaporation occurred, thereby making the most efficient use of the hot containers and the fuel used to heat them.[2]

At Big Bone Lick, the earliest record of salt manufacture is from 1755. In the autumn of that year, according to John Ingles, a party of "Indians started to the Bigg Bone lick which is now in the state of Kentuckey and took my mother & severale other of the prisoners to make salt." His mother was Mary Draper Ingles, who had been captured the previous summer during a Shawnee raid into present-day Virginia. The raiding party took Mrs. Ingles and other captives down the Kanawha Valley on the way to the Shawnee village at what is now Portsmouth, Ohio. Ingles's description of his mother's journey to the village includes an interval of salt gathering along the shore of the Kanawha River:

> They still worked on in this way until they got down some little Distance above the mouth of the great Kanawa They came to a little salt spring in the Bank of the river the Indians stoped there and rested for a day or two there & with what kittles they Had with them boiled & mad some salt Then they started on from there & persued this journey until they got to the nation where the Indians lived which was at the mouth of the Bigg Sioto.

Mary Ingles was separated from the other captives a short time after arriving at the Shawnee village. Between performing her assigned duties at the village that summer, she made shirts from fabric sold by French traders at the Shawnee settlement, exchanging the garments for money and other goods. Such traders were likely the source of the iron kettles that were displacing the Indians' traditional ceramic salt pans.

In the autumn of 1755, Ingles and another woman were among the prisoners taken to collect salt at Big Bone Lick. At the Lick, they made a daring escape from their Shawnee captors and hiked eastward in increasingly colder weather for forty days. (Part of the path the women traveled is now Kentucky Route 8, or Mary Ingles Highway.) The exhausted women were finally found and rescued by a man who had known Ingles for many years. A decade later, Mary Ingles gave birth to John, who later recorded his mother's narrative of her captivity and escape.[3]

Native Americans almost certainly gathered salt at Big Bone Lick prior to Mary Ingles's visit. Hundreds of years earlier, the Indians in the region had begun to consume quantities of maize, beans, and squash, likely causing their diets to become deficient in salt. Ceramic salt pans have been unearthed from prehistoric village sites located within twenty-five miles of Big Bone Lick, and prehistoric fire pits and boiling pits (the latter used to hold water in which hot rocks were placed) uncovered at the Lick may have been used to evaporate brine. However, prehistoric Indian artifacts definitively associated with salt processing have not yet been found at the springs, making the mid-eighteenth century the earliest period for which there is concrete evidence of Indian salt-making activity at the Lick.[4]

Those Indians that cultivated plants did not domesticate animals. They procured meat primarily by killing native herbivores (white-tailed deer, elk, and American bison) that foraged in the forests and meadows and visited licks for salt. In contrast, the Old World meat animals (cattle, pigs, sheep, and goats) introduced by immigrants were generally restricted to farms and had to have their salt brought to them. The eighteenth-century introduction of these domesticated herbivores to the Ohio Valley created a new need for the salt manufactured from saline springs.[5]

The early pioneers in Kentucky, Ohio, and Indiana further increased the demand for salt through their use of the mineral in making soap, manufacturing leather, dyeing fabric, and producing cheese. Above all else, the settlers employed salt for meat preservation, a use not practiced in Native American cultures. From the late eighteenth through mid-nineteenth centuries, the primary export of the Cincinnati region was salted meat, mostly pork, which was shipped over the Ohio River.[6]

The economic importance of salt can be gauged by Big Bone Lick's high real estate value. The first owner of the Lick and the surrounding land was William Christian, who was granted the property in 1779 in recognition of his service as a soldier in the Seven Years' (or French and Indian) War. At the time, Kentucky was a county of Virginia, so Christian received the military grant from Virginia's governor, Thomas Jefferson. The potential profitability of the Lick's salt springs allowed Christian to sell his 1,000-acre tract in 1780 for 1,350 pounds—almost six times the selling price of a neighboring tract of the same size that lacked springs. David Ross was the buyer, and he later added another 1,000 acres through the purchase of adjacent real estate. Ross had his partner and agents make salt at the Lick, but he also leased property at the springs to other salt manufacturers.[7]

A small fortification (the "Old Fort" in figure 4) was built at the Lick to protect the salt workers and their equipment from Indian raids, and eighteen soldiers were posted there in 1790. During this period, the salt makers switched to smaller kettles when they discovered that faster evaporation produced larger salt yields. Thirty-five-gallon containers became the norm, since that volume of water could be quickly boiled away. An advertisement in the March 3, 1792, issue of the *Kentucky Gazette* offered to rent out a saltworks at Big Bone Lick consisting of more than 100 thirty-five-gallon pans, along with nine wagons and gear. The "good old Kentucky salt" offered for sale in a 1794 Cincinnati advertisement may have been gathered at Big Bone Lick or, less likely, at one of Kentucky's other licks.[8]

Salt making at the Lick continued during the first years of

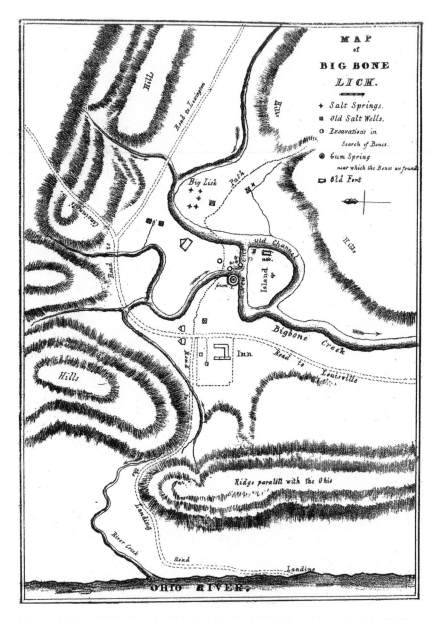

Figure 4. Map of Big Bone Lick in 1830, oriented with north to the left. (William Cooper, "Notices of Big-Bone Lick," *Monthly American Journal of Geology and Natural Science* 1 [1831]: 169)

the nineteenth century. In 1808, David Ross settled a portion of a debt by deeding his 2,000 acres along Big Bone Creek to three Virginians. By 1810, a Scotsman by the name of Colquohoun had come into ownership of the Lick, where he produced about sixty bushels of salt per day from two salt furnaces. Colquohoun's innovative furnace design was described in detail by Zadok Cramer in 1811:

> Mr. Colquohoun has been at much labor and expense in fixing his furnaces in a superior stile, particularly in the retention of heat, and saving the fuel. His kettles are of an oblong square, coming to about half the size at bottom that they are at the top; they hold about 12 or 15 gals., and are fixed close together in a double row, having their edges covered with sheet lead lapped down closely on all sides, so as to prevent any heat from escaping; the fuel is introduced into a grated furnace, whose mouth is closed by an iron door.—The kettles rise gradually from the front to the chimney, so as to occasion a sufficient draught of air. The first kettle in the furnace is round and contains about 100 gallons, and as this receives the greatest degree of heat, and evaporates the water much faster than the smaller ones, they are partly supplied from it after the water has boiled down considerable, and the small black kettles are supplied from those near the front.[9]

Despite the efficiency of the furnaces, salt makers at Big Bone Lick could not match the cheaper cost of salt production at many of the more recently developed salt springs in the Ohio Valley. The problem lay in the weakness of the Lick's brine—between 500 and 1,000 gallons of salt water had to be evaporated to produce a bushel of salt. At other springs, salt makers could collect a bushel of salt from as little as 50 gallons of brine, making their fuel and labor costs much lower than those at Big Bone Lick.

Figure 5. William Clark noted that farm animals
were attracted to the springs at Big Bone Lick.
(Library of Congress, Prints and Photographs
Division)

Because of market competition from the more productive saltworks, salt gathering at the Lick ceased in 1812.[10]

Even after salt collection stopped at Big Bone Lick, animals
from neighboring farms continued to consume its saline spring
water. The local livestock's attraction to the brine was noted in
an 1807 letter to President Thomas Jefferson from William
Clark (figure 5), co-leader of the recently completed Lewis and
Clark expedition. Clark wrote, "Dureing the three weeks I remained at the Big-bone Lick, I observed every day great Num-

bers of the Nighbours Cattle and horses, and sometimes hogs eagerly Comeing into the Lick and drinking an emence quantity of the water." According to Clark, the Lick's neighbors believed "there was something in the air about the Lick very agreeable to the Cattle, and observed, that the[y] Came from every direction for six or eight Miles arround to that Place to drink the Salt water, and further observed that a drove of Cattle on their way from the interior settlement to be Pastered Near that Place, when in 2 and a half miles of the Lick they became restless and ran with eagerness to the Place and drank profusely of the water."[11]

In addition to providing salt for animals and people, the Lick's brine was used for medicinal purposes. John Filson published the earliest notice of the brine's curative properties in 1784: "A medicinal spring is found near Big-bone Lick, which has perfectly cured the itch by once bathing; and experience in time may discover in it other virtues." To take advantage of the public's interest in drinking and bathing in the healthful mineral waters, an inn known as the Clay House (in honor of Kentucky statesman Henry Clay) was built west of the Lick during the early nineteenth century (see figure 4). Bathhouses and a pavilion with seats were erected at the spring located nearest the inn. People traveled to the health resort, according to one guest, "to loiter, drink, bathe, and kill the game—very plenty yet on the hills." Another visitor praised the inn's owner more than the wooded surroundings: "The land about it is flat and cold, with scrubby timber, and there is no cleared ground in view of the Lick, not even a garden; notwithstanding, it is worth a visit to the curious, and the superior intelligence and hospitality of its worthy proprietor makes such a visit well paid for."[12]

In 1815, renowned frontier physician Daniel Drake detailed the contents of the curative spring waters: "The waters of Big Bone hold in solution, besides common salt, the *muriate of lime*, *sulphate of soda* or *magnesia*, and a few other salts of less activity."

In addition, the fifty-seven-degree spring waters "afford a great quantity of *sulphurated hydrogen gas*, which is constantly escaping in bubbles." Drake described the taste and smell of the springs as "sulphurous, and offensive to strangers; but the impression made by the gas is transient, and the taste of the common salt afterwards predominates." Drake recommended using the medicinal waters to combat specific illnesses: "The disorders to which they seem particularly adapted, are the torpor, obstruction or chronic inflammation produced by acute diseases in the lungs, liver, spleen, kidnies, in short, any of the viscera." For treating such illnesses, Drake believed, the spring waters at Big Bone Lick were as good as the mineral waters found anywhere else. He prescribed drinking a pint to a gallon daily, "according to the strength of the patient, and its sensible effects on the system."[13]

In a later paper on healthful mineral springs, Drake objected to the gamblers and gambling machines at spas such as the Lick's Clay House: "They call off the attention of husbands, fathers, and brothers, from those whom they had conducted thither for health; they draw the unwary into their snares with the greater facility, because of the idleness which prevails at such places." According to Drake, just the rumor of gambling "is offensive to the taste and feelings, of moral and religious invalids; and has often banished them from the springs, before a proper trial was completed." Drake's criticism likely had no effect on the prevalence of gambling, which was a valued component of the social life at many of Kentucky's health resorts.[14]

The original Clay House was consumed by fire in the mid-1840s, and in 1848, Judge Lewis Collins of Maysville, Kentucky, noted that "the springs at this place have been considerably frequented on account of their medicinal values; but at this time no accommodation of any sort for visiters is kept there, and but very inadequate accommodation is to be found any where in the neighborhood." Sometime after Collins's report, a new Clay

House was built just north of the Lick along the road to Cincinnati. This health resort was repaired and refurnished after the Civil War, and in 1866 its owners advertised, "Big Bone water is unsurpassed for its invigorating qualities, as has been attested by hundreds who have been restored to health by its use." In 1874, Richard Collins revised his father's earlier report on the Lick, noting that more lodging had been erected recently, "and the accommodations are now excellent." The younger Collins also reported on an interesting discovery made during an upgrade of the facilities for barreling the Lick's water for sale. While excavating for the project, workers unearthed a wagonload of animal remains, including elephantine vertebrae, a twelve-foot-long tusk, and a twenty-pound tooth.[15]

In May 1876, John Campbell distributed 2,000 posters announcing his acquisition of the Clay House. The *Boone County Recorder* subsequently ran an article recommending the hotel: "We would say to all those wishing to spend the warm summer months at one of the best medical springs in this country, and at reasonable rates, go to Big Bone Springs and take lodging at the Clay House." At the end of the summer of 1876, a satisfied hotel guest wrote, "there is an exhilarating and invigorating sensation experienced during and after a bath that is almost indescribable." He also noted that many local citizens visited the Lick daily "to get their nip of sulphur water (for they cannot, for love or money, get anything stronger in this precinct, Local Option having carried at the August election)."[16]

In 1881, new owner C. A. McLaughlin Jr. placed advertisements in local newspapers announcing the renovation of the hotel:

This popular resort, which has been entirely refitted, will be open for the reception of guests May 10th. Every arrangement has been made to insure the pleasure and comfort of visitors. The Sulphur Baths can be taken hot or cold. Terms—$7 to $9 per week. Special rates can be obtained for families wishing to spend a longer time than one week. Big Bone can be reached by taking the 3 o'clock, p.m., Madison packet, at Mail-boat Landing, Cincinnati, which lands at Hamilton, where an omnibus will meet the boat every day.[17]

At least three medical doctors resided at the Lick in 1883, one of whom advertised in a northern Kentucky atlas:

Dr. J. E. Stevenson, Propr. of Hotel for Invalids. Waters unsurpassed. Big Bone Springs, Ky. A Physician of thirty-eight years' experience. Special attention shown to all who visit these springs for cures. Also a pleasant resort for those desiring sport. P.O., Hamilton, Ky.[18]

At a medical society meeting at Big Bone Lick in 1894, Dr. Myrax J. Crouch of nearby Union, Kentucky, reported that the spring waters were especially useful in combating certain health problems. Taken internally, the waters helped in the prevention and treatment of tuberculosis, rheumatism, uterine trouble, hemorrhoids, lead poisoning, and boils. External application of the waters cured parasitic skin diseases, washed off chemical pollutants, acted as "a useful hair tonic," and provided "a peculiarly stimulating bath."[19]

In the early 1900s, with the introduction of effective drugs and new amusements such as automobiles and moving picture shows, most Kentucky health resorts went out of business. The hotel at Big Bone Lick operated into the first decade of the twentieth century, after which the building fell into disrepair. In 1916, the newly founded Big Bone Spring Company formulated plans to provide modern accommodations, but nothing came of the venture. The old hotel was dismantled for scrap lumber in 1945, eliminating the last vestige of the days when humans were attracted to the Lick for its salty and curative waters. The Lick's big bones, however, continued to draw people to the site.[20]

Chapter 3

—— ❧ ——

Indian Accounts of Great Buffalo

West from the springs by a gradual and easy ascent, rises the Indian hill, from the top of which there is an extensive view of the surrounding country. It was from this spot, according to Indian tradition, that the last great Mammoth Bull, stricken and scorched by heaven's lightning, bolted and made his wondrous leap over the Wabash, the lakes and to his present home.
—*Licking Valley Register*, March 13, 1847

Beginning in the mid-1700s, frontier soldiers, surveyors, and traders removed large bones, tusks, and teeth from Big Bone Lick and carried them to the seaboard colonies and on to Europe. The uniqueness of the fossils caused American and European scientists to become curious about their site of discovery. For example, when Philadelphia botanist John Bartram was notified in 1762 that a Shawnee party had brought an elephantine tooth and a broken tusk to Fort Pitt in Pittsburgh, he asked western Pennsylvania naturalist James Wright to inquire about where the skeletal materials had been found. Wright's lengthy written reply to Bartram contains the earliest detailed description of Big Bone Lick, the origin of the large remains:

Pursuant to thy request, I have made as particular an Enquiry relating to those bones thou mentions, as I possibly

Could, from two Sencible Shawanese Indians, Assisted by an Interpreter, And the Substance of what they Say is as follows—the place where they lye is about 3 miles from the Ohio, salt & moist, as well as I could judge by their description of it seems to contain 30 or 40 Acres, in the Midst of a large Savannah, 4 days Journey Below the lower Shawanese town, on the East Side of the river, that there appear to be the remains of 5 Entire Sceletons, with their heads All Pointing towards Each other, And near together, supposed to have fallen at the same time; . . . they were asked if they had seen those long bones they Call'd horns, they Answered they had, And by the distance from where they stood to the door, Showd them to be 10 or 12 feet long, And added that by the Bones, they Judged the Creature when Alive must have been the Size of a Small house, pointing from the Window to a Stable in Sight;—I askd them if the Place where they lay was Surounded with Mountains, So as to admit a probability of its Ever having been a lake, they Answered, the place was salt and Wettish, And by having been much trod & Licked, was somthing lower then the adjacent land, which however, was so level, to a prodigious Extent, that the lick, as they Calld it, Could never have been coverd with water; And that there were many roads thro this Extent of land, larger & more beaten by Buffalas and other Creatures, that had made them to go to it, than any Roads they saw in this Part of the Country.[1]

Thus, the Shawnee had found the big bones, teeth, and horns (actually tusks) at what they called a "lick," an area where wet, salty soil was licked and trod upon by bison, elk, and deer. Hundreds of these licks were scattered across the Ohio Valley, but few were as extensive or attracted as many animals as Big Bone Lick. All early accounts of the site depict it as a large area

Figure 6. American bison reached Big Bone Lick via established paths through the forest. (John D. Godman, *American Natural History*, 2nd ed. [1831], pt. 1, vol. 3, p. 4)

of bare dirt depressed three to four feet below the floor of the wooded Big Bone Creek valley. The licking, stamping, and burrowing of salt-seeking mammals, especially the abundant bison (figure 6), were responsible for creating the depression.[2]

At least four bison roads (or buffalo traces), each up to fifteen feet wide, led through the forest to Big Bone Lick. Herds approaching from the west swam across the Ohio River to the mouth of Big Bone Creek and then proceeded to the Lick by walking upstream along a bison road that paralleled the creek. Animals converging from the north crossed the Ohio at the future site of Cincinnati and then continued southward on a bison path leading to the Lick. Animals also reached the site via bison roads from the southeast and the southwest. Indians often visited the Lick to hunt and to procure salt, and they too traveled on these roads that had been cleared and beaten down by the bison.[3]

There are several Indian narratives concerning the big bones they found at the site. For example, at the conclusion of Wright's

1762 meeting with the Shawnee, his guests related a story that explained the disappearance of the species represented by the five animal skeletons found at Big Bone Lick:

> I Askd if they had Ever heard from their old men, when these 5 were first observed, or if they, or their fathers, had Ever seen any such large Creatures living, as these bones were supposd to have been a part of, they Answered they had never heard them spoken of, other then as in the Condition they are at present, nor ever heard of any such creature having been seen by the oldest Man, or his father—that they had indeed a tradition, such mighty Creatures, once frequented those Savannahs, that there were then men of a size proportionable to them, who used to kill them, and tye them in Their hoppisses [back straps] And throw them upon their Backs As an Indian now dos a Deer, that they had seen Marks in the rocks, which tradition said, were made by these Great & Strong Men, when they sate down with their Burthens, such as a Man makes by sitting down on the Snow, that when there were no more of these strong Men left alive, God Kiled these Mighty Creatures, that they should not hurt the Present race of Indians, And added, God had Kill'd these last 5 they had been questioned about, which the Interpreter said was to be understood, they supposed them to have been Killd by lightning— these the Shawanese said were their traditions, and as to what they knew, they had told it.[4]

The Shawnee story contains many elements that were common in traditional Indian narratives, but the reference to God was likely a more recent alteration. In original Indian cosmologies, supernatural power was apportioned among various earth, sky, and water spirits. The appearance of a single powerful God or "Great Spirit" in eighteenth-century Indian legends was the result of the incorporation of Christian beliefs into Native American theologies.[5]

In 1766, four years after Wright heard the aforementioned story at Pittsburgh, an Indian chief visiting the Lick offered an alternative explanation for the presence of the big bones. That year, Indian agent George Croghan led a large flotilla down the Ohio River on a journey from Pittsburgh to the Illinois country, and they stopped at Big Bone Lick (see chapter 4 for more details). Members of Croghan's party included Indian warriors, British military men, and Indian trader George Morgan, and at least Croghan and Morgan collected some of the large bones, teeth, and tusks lying about the Lick.[6] While at the site, Morgan spoke with the chief of an Iroquois and Wyandot war party headed south to battle the Chickasaw. The eighty-four-year-old chief revealed that he had visited the Lick on many occasions: "Whilst I was yet a boy I passed this road several times, to war against the Catawbas; and the wise old chiefs, among whom was my grandfather, then gave me the tradition, handed down to us, respecting these bones, the like to which are found in no other part of the country." The chief then related the legend explaining the site's unique skeletal remains:

After the Great Spirit first formed the world, he made the various birds and beasts which now inhabit it. He also made man; but having formed him very white, and imperfect, and ill-tempered he placed him on one side of it where he now inhabits, and from whence he has lately found a passage across the great water, to be a plague to us. As the Great Spirit was not pleased with this his work, he took of black clay, and made what *you* call a negro, with a woolly head. This black man was much better than the white man, but still he did not answer the wish of the Great Spirit, that is, he was imperfect; at last, the Great Spirit having procured a piece of pure, fine red clay, formed from it the Red Man, perfectly to his mind; and he was so well pleased with him, that he placed him on this great island, separate from the white and black men, and gave him rules for his conduct, promising happiness in proportion as they should be observed. He increased exceedingly, and was perfectly happy for ages; but the foolish young people, at length forgetting his rules, became exceedingly ill-tempered and wicked. In consequence of this, the Great Spirit created the great buffalo, the bones of which you now see before us; these made war upon the human species alone, and destroyed all but a few, who repented and promised the Great Spirit to live according to his laws, if he would restrain the devouring enemy; whereupon he sent thunder and lightning, and destroyed the whole race, in this spot, two excepted, a male and a female, which he shut up in yonder mountain, ready to let loose again, should occasion require.[7]

It is likely that the part of the story about the human races had been added after the northeastern Indians learned about the geography of the world. It was not uncommon for Native Americans to incorporate new knowledge when retelling a narrative, especially when the additional information could be embellished to reflect Indian superiority. The remainder of the chief's tale—that the Lick's large bones were those of the homicidal great buffalo—had probably been repeated for many generations.[8]

Even before the chief told his story in 1766, American and European naturalists were aware that the Indians attributed the big bones to a huge bison species. For example, in a 1762 letter to John Bartram, Englishman Peter Collinson asked for more information on the "Great Buffalo" whose remains "are now standing in a Licking place not far from the Ohio." The Native Americans' belief was based on their misidentification of scat-

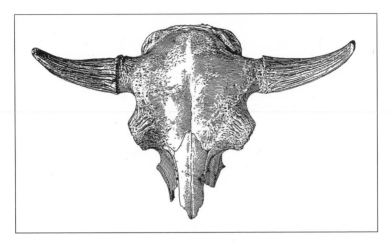

Figure 7. Bison horns are shaped like tusks, explaining why the Lick's big tusks were misidentified as great buffalo horns. (Oliver P. Hay, "The Pleistocene Period and Its Vertebrata," *Thirty-sixth Annual Report of Indiana Department of Geology and Natural Resources* [1911], 650)

tered elephantine tusks as being the horns of enormous buffalo. Proboscidean tusks were unknown to Native Americans, but they were very well acquainted with bison horns (figure 7).[9]

In a third Indian narrative concerning the big bones, the fearsome creature of the Lick was identified as a massive beast that threatened to destroy the Indians' animal resources. Thomas Jefferson heard this legend sometime between 1775 and 1781, at a council he held with a delegation of Delaware warriors. According to Jefferson's description of the meeting, when he asked the Indians what they knew about the large animal whose remains had been found at Big Bone Lick:

> Their chief speaker immediately put himself into an attitude of oratory, and with a pomp suited to what he conceived the elevation of his subject, informed him [Jefferson] that it was a tradition handed down from their fathers, "That in antient times a herd of these tremendous animals

came to the Big-bone licks, and began an universal destruction of the bear, deer, elks, buffaloes, and other animals, which had been created for the use of the Indians: that the Great Man above, looking down and seeing this, was so enraged that he seized his lightning, descended on the earth, seated himself on a neighboring mountain, on a rock, of which his seat and the print of his feet are still to be seen, and hurled his bolts among them till the whole were slaughtered, except the big bull, who presenting his forehead to the shafts, shook them off as they fell; but missing one at length, it wounded him in the side; whereon, springing round, he bounded over the Ohio, over the Wabash, the Illinois, and finally over the great lakes, where he is living at this day."[10]

Thus, according to all three Indian narratives quoted in this chapter, the Lick's big bones are the remains of monstrous animals that were struck dead by spirit-propelled lightning bolts. In contrast, in an Iroquois account of the animals' demise, neither lightning nor a sky spirit played a part in the death of the beasts. Instead, the large bison at the Lick were killed by arrows shot from the bows of pygmies. Ethnologist Erminnie Smith recorded this Iroquois story in the mid-1800s:

It was customary for the Iroquois tribes to make raids upon the Cherokees while the latter inhabited the swamps of Florida [the eighteenth-century name for most of the Southeast].

One of these raiding parties had been away from home about two years, and on the very evening of the journey homeward one of its number was taken quite ill. After a long consultation (the man continuing to grow worse), the party concluded to leave him, and when they had reached one of the rivers of the Alleghany Mountains they abandoned him on the shore. After their arrival at home the warriors were questioned in regard to the missing war-chief. In reply, they said that they did not exactly know what had become of him, and that he must have been lost or killed in the "Southern country."

During the night the sick chief lying on the bank heard the soft sounds of a canoe's approach, and saw three male pigmies landing hurriedly. Finding him, they bade him to lie there until they returned, as they were going to a neighboring "salt-lick" where many strange animals watered, and where they were to watch for some of them to come up out of the earth.

Reaching the place the pigmies found that the animals had not come out from the ground. They hid themselves and soon saw a male buffalo approach. The beast looked around and began to drink, and immediately two buffalo cows arose out of the lick.

The three animals, after quenching their thirst, lay down upon the bank.

The pigmies seeing that the animals were becoming restless and uneasy, concluded wisely to shoot them, and succeeded in killing the two buffalo cows.

They returned to the man and told him that they would care for him. This they did, and brought him to his friends, who from his story learned that the returned warriors were false, and they were accordingly punished.

From a strong desire to see the "lick," a large party searched for it and found it surrounded with bones of various large animals killed by the pigmies.[11]

A Wyandot storyteller shared a similar legend during the latter half of the nineteenth century. In this tale, the springs at Big Bone Lick were once dominated by Witch Buffalo, massive female bison that drove away the animals hunted by the Indians.

Luckily, Little People arrived and slaughtered the enormous Witch Buffalo, leaving their big bones scattered around the springs. Such elflike folk appear in many northeastern Indian stories, standing guard over ripening fruits, assisting hunters in the pursuit of game, and destroying monstrous creatures with their arrows. The beloved elves, according to Onondaga Wesleyan minister Thomas La Fort, "used to be frequent in the old times, the little men being often seen, helping men, but since Christianity had prevailed they had disappeared."[12]

Finally, there is written evidence of other Indian legends concerning the Lick's big bones. These stories were mentioned briefly in the 1775 journal of Nicholas Cresswell, a British member of a contentious Ohio River party that stopped at the flooded Lick to procure some meat:

> Our company quarreled and the Irishman left us and went to Cresop's people [a group of Virginia militiamen accompanying them], but returned to us at the Bone Lick where we camped. . . . Joseph Passiers found a jaw tooth which he gave me. It was judged by the company to weigh 10 pound. I got a shell of a Tusk of hard and good ivory about eighteen inches long. There is a great number of bones in a Bank on the side of this pond of enormous size but decayed and rotten. Ribs 9 inches broad, Thigh bones 10 inches diameter. What sort of animals these were is not clearly known. All the traditionary accounts by the Indians is that they were White Buffaloes that killed themselves by drinking salt water.

Following this reference to otherwise unknown Indian accounts of the source of the big bones, Cresswell's journal entry concludes by touching on many aspects of the Lick that have been mentioned in this chapter, including the occurrence of lightning strikes at the location:

Saw some buffalos but killed none. Several Indian paintings on the trees. Got plenty of Mulberries, very sweet and pleasant fruit but bad for the teeth. One of the company shot a Deer. The loudest Thunder and heaviest rain I ever saw this afternoon. Got to camp well wet and most heartily tired. A D—d Irish rascal has broken a piece of my Elephant tooth, put me in a violent passion, can write no more.[13]

On the basis of descriptions of the site and specimens collected by visitors such as Croghan, Morgan, and Cresswell, American and European anatomists eventually decided that Big Bone Lick's large fossils were the remains of neither enormous bison nor elephants. Scientists thus struggled to correctly identify the Lick's big-boned species.

Chapter 4

∽

Gathering the Bones

[Concerning the molars, tusk, and femur carried to France
from Big Bone Lick,] it can never be supposed that these
teeth could have been taken from the same head with the
tusks, or that they could have made part of the same skeleton with the femur above-mentioned.
—Georges-Louis Leclerc de Buffon, 1762

Early-eighteenth-century French and British fur traders competed to establish trading networks in the Ohio Valley. France
claimed ownership of the entire Mississippi River drainage system and looked on English, Scottish, and Irish traders from the
Atlantic seaboard colonies as trespassers. However, enforcement of France's territorial claim proved difficult in the vast
interior wilderness, and many British traders were able to disperse into the Ohio Valley. France also faced a problem in the
South, where local Indians opposed any European presence.[1]

In the Lower Mississippi Valley, the Chickasaw Indian nation disrupted communication between France's colonies in
Canada and Louisiana. The Indians attacked the boats of French
soldiers and traders on the Mississippi River, and they blocked
the northward migration of French colonists from New Orleans. As part of an effort to subdue the hostile Chickasaw, the
governor of Louisiana arranged to have the governor of Canada

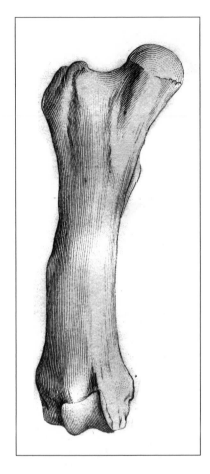

Figure 8. Forty-inch-long femur collected at Big Bone Lick in 1739. (Georges Cuvier, *Recherches sur les ossemens fossiles*, 3rd ed. [1825], vol. 1, p. 248, plate 4)

send a military force south from Montreal in 1739. Baron Charles de Longueuil was in command of the expedition, which set off in boats at the end of June. One of Longueuil's officers was seventeen-year-old assistant engineer Joseph-Gaspard Chaussegros de Lery, whose primary responsibility was to record the route of the expedition through the uncharted Ohio Valley. The 442-man party included 319 Indian warriors in addition to French and Canadian militia members. The flotilla was reinforced by additional Indians, including Shawnee, as it descended the Ohio

River that summer. Upon reaching the vicinity of Big Bone Lick, a site well known to the Indians, Longueuil planted the banner of the king of France, claiming the region for that country. Longueuil also gathered an assortment of fossil skeletal remains from the Lick.

Longueuil's army continued downstream to the Mississippi River, joined up with other French militias, and began to move against the Chickasaw in February 1740. The campaign concluded in April, but Longueuil did not accompany his troops back to Canada. Instead, he continued down the Mississippi River to New Orleans and eventually sailed to France from that port at the end of the year. Longueuil carried some of the Big Bone Lick fossils with him across the Atlantic. Upon reaching France, he deposited an enormous femur (figure 8), a tusk, and three molar teeth in the Cabinet du Roi, a collection of curiosities located in the chateau of the king's botanical garden, the Jardin du Roi.[2]

In 1740, Louisiana militiaman Philippe Mandeville used Lery's trip log from the Longueuil expedition to draft a rough map of the Ohio River. The map bore the following inscription (in French) at the approximate location of Big Bone Lick: "Place where the bones of many elephants were found by the army from Canada commanded by the Baron de Longuille, and where he had the Arms of the King set up in 1739." Unfortunately, when the notation of the Lick's site was reworded on Jacques Nicolas Bellin's 1744 map of interior eastern North America, it read (in French): "Place where elephant bones were found in 1729" (figure 9). Because of this transcription error (perhaps caused by a blurred number on the Mandeville map), many published accounts have mistakenly listed 1729 as the year of Longueuil's acquisition of fossils from Big Bone Lick.[3]

Other historians have identified 1735 as the year when a Canadian military party first observed skeletal remains at Big Bone Lick. This date is taken from a letter written in 1756 by Jean-

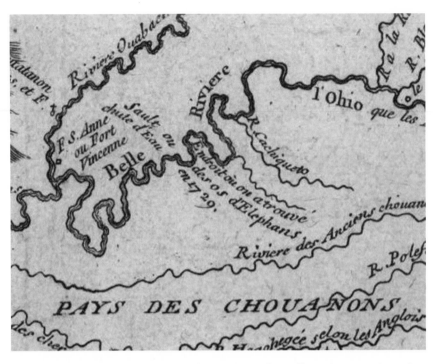

Figure 9. Detail from 1755 edition of Jacques Nicolas Bellin's 1744 map *Carte de la Louisiane etc.* (Library of Congress, Geography and Map Division)

Bernard Bossu, a French officer who served in America from 1751 to 1762. According to Bossu, "In 1735, the Canadians, who had come to fight the Chickasaws, discovered the skeletons of seven elephants in the vicinity of the Belle, or Ohio, River." Either Bossu was mistaken about the year of Longueuil's expedition, or soldiers had actually been sent from Canada in 1735 to participate in French actions against the Chickasaw. Bossu assumed that the bones found at the Lick were from elephants that had originated in the Old World. He believed that, from Asia, a small herd of "animals must have wandered off on dry land and through the forests to this new continent." The elephants then traveled through the West to their demise at the

Lick, "a swamp into which they sank up to their bellies because of their enormous weight and from which they were unable to extricate themselves." Bossu likely became interested in the deceased animals after he received a six-and-a-half-pound molar from an Indian who had found it along with other large teeth at the Lick.[4]

In the same year that Bossu was writing his letter in America, two drawings of a molar from Longueuil's collection were published in Paris (figure 10). These illustrations, the first pictures of an American vertebrate fossil, appeared in a paper by mineralogist Jean-Étienne Guettard comparing the geology of North America with that of Switzerland. Along with the diagrams of the molar, Guettard described the tooth and referred to the site of its discovery as "the place where the elephant bones were found." Guettard, however, did not identify the fossil as the molar of an elephant; instead, he left the reader with the question, "What animal does it come from?" Guettard did not believe that the tooth came from an elephant because the molar's chewing surface was composed of conical knobs—a marked contrast to the parallel low ridges of an elephant molar (figure 11). Also, the tooth from Big Bone Lick was covered with dense enamel, whereas the surface of an elephant tooth has relatively little enamel.[5]

In 1762, Louis Jean-Marie Daubenton, a zoologist at the Jardin du Roi, reported that he had examined all five fossils in Longueuil's collection from Big Bone Lick and compared them with the corresponding anatomical structures of an elephant. He concluded that the femur and tusk from the Lick were those of a large elephant, but the three knobby molars came from a gigantic hippopotamus. According to Daubenton, the materials taken from the Lick were apparently the commingled remains of two mammals—an enormous hippopotamus and a very big elephant that he called "the animal of the Ohio." Anatomical comparisons also led Daubenton to determine that the animal

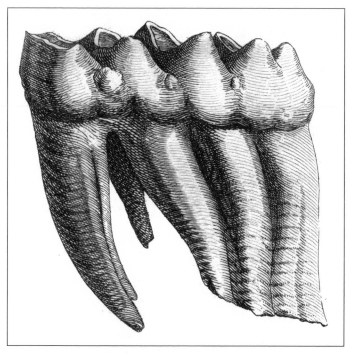

Figure 10. Molar collected at Big Bone Lick in 1739 and described in Paris in 1756. (Georges Cuvier, *Recherches sur les ossemens fossiles,* 3rd ed. [1825], vol. 1, p. 248, plate 1)

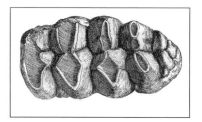 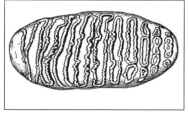

Figure 11. Surface view of the molar illustrated in figure 10 (left) and the molar of an Asian elephant (right). (Georges Cuvier, *Recherches sur les ossemens fossiles,* 3rd ed. [1825], vol. 1, p. 248, plate 1; Richard Lydekker, *Catalogue of the Ungulate Mammals in the British Museum* [1916], vol. 5, p. 80)

known as the Siberian mammoth was nothing more than an oversized elephant, a conclusion that had already been reached by British and German anatomists. European scientists had first learned of the Siberian mammoth during the previous century when they began receiving accounts of its fossil remains from Asia. The European term *mammoth* was a transliteration of *mammut*, the Siberian name for the animal whose fossil ivory tusks were fashioned into utensils by native peoples or exported south to China.[6]

Today, we know that the Siberian (or woolly) mammoth was a unique proboscidean species that became extinct, but Daubenton and the great majority of his colleagues rejected the idea of extinction. For them, all animals had been created by God and were destined to exist in unchanged perfection until the end of time. Therefore, even though a fossil femur of a Siberian mammoth did not look the same as the femur of an elephant, Daubenton's religious views forced him to conclude that the Siberian mammoth's femur was merely a variant of the elephant's normal femur. It was inconceivable to Daubenton that a fossil femur could be the bone of a species that had vanished.

In the case of the fossil remains from Big Bone Lick, both the femur and the tusk of the animal of the Ohio were clearly different from those structures on an elephant. However, as in the case of the Siberian mammoth, Daubenton's personal beliefs led him to conclude that the animal of the Ohio was simply a large elephant. The Lick's fossil teeth, however, certainly were not variants of elephant molars. The knobby teeth more closely resembled the molars of a hippopotamus, which Daubenton took as their source. It would have been impossible for him to surmise that a species with hippopotamus-like molars and elephantine bones and tusks had once existed. As paleontologist George Gaylord Simpson later wrote, the limits of Daubenton's "scientific imagination, or that of any of his learned contemporaries, had been reached."[7]

Naturalist Georges-Louis Leclerc de Buffon, Daubenton's superior at the Jardin du Roi, also divided Longueuil's Big Bone Lick fossils between two species—the hippopotamus and an elephant-like mammoth. Buffon used the term *mammoth* to designate both the Siberian mammoth and the animal of the Ohio. He believed that those two creatures were simply the Old and New World representatives of the mammoth, a northern species that had lived at a time when tropical temperatures extended into the world's higher latitudes. According to Buffon, the mammoth "no longer exists anywhere," its extinction having been caused by the cooling earth.[8]

Buffon's first reference to vanished species appeared in 1749, when he wrote that many marine invertebrates had disappeared. His assertion of extinction was surprising, since it ran counter to the prevailing Judeo-Christian belief in a perfect, unchanging creation. In 1764, French religious authorities must have been pleased when Buffon rescinded his earlier declaration that a species known as the mammoth had become extinct. Instead, Buffon adopted Daubenton's view that the Siberian mammoth and the animal of the Ohio were both northern forms of the extant elephant rather than a vanished species.[9]

As Longueuil's specimens were being studied in Paris, parties arriving at Big Bone Lick continued to view and gather fossils from the site. A Frenchman by the name of Fabri was likely at the Lick in the 1740s when he saw "heads and skeletons of an enormous quadruped, called by the Savages the *father of oxen*." Pennsylvania Indian trader Robert Smith collected remains at the Lick, including a tusk that he hid in a stream "at some Distance from the Place, lest French Indians should carry it away." In 1751, Smith had his workers convey two large teeth to Christopher Gist, a land surveyor who was working nearby. Gist, in turn, gave his Virginia employer one of the teeth, which weighed more than four pounds and "looked like fine Ivory when the outside was scraped off."[10]

Pennsylvania Indian trader John Findley (or Finley) may have accompanied a group of Shawnee on a 1752 visit to the Lick. And in 1755, Mary Ingles fled from her Shawnee captors, who had taken her to gather salt at the site (see chapter 2). In her son's narrative of her ordeal, he wrote, "I have frequantly Heard my mother say when she left the lick that she exchanged her tomehock with one of three Frenchmen who was all sitting on One of the large Bones that was there and cracking walnuts."[11]

Also in 1755, Philadelphia cartographer Lewis Evans published *A General Map of the Middle British Colonies, in America; etc.* and designated the Lick's location near the Ohio River with the label "Elephants Bones found here." The map of English holdings included the Ohio River because, according to the British, the Iroquois had granted England total control of the Ohio Valley in 1744. France's rejection of the British claim culminated in the Seven Years' War that began in 1756 and ended in 1763, when victorious England was given possession of all land east of the Mississippi River, with the exception of New Orleans and a small outlying area.[12]

Toward the end of the Seven Years' War, James Kenny was put in charge of the trading store run by the Pennsylvania Commission of Indian Affairs in Pittsburgh. There, he learned about Big Bone Lick from the visiting Indians and frontier travelers. In his 1762 journal, Kenny stated his opinion "that this Continent Produces Eliphants, as large Teeth have been found in a Lick down ye Ohio between 4 & 6 lb weight, one of which I seen Weigh'd, which Weighed 4¼ lb." Kenny also heard "that there are some Teeth too heavy to be carried, that there are Horns about 12 foot Long, as I suppose is ye Eye teeth of Elephants." In 1763, Kenny recorded an alternative interpretation of the Lick's remains by hunter and trapper Benjamin Sutton, who had seen some teeth weighing more than seven pounds and nine shoulder blades up to a yard wide. Sutton identified the remains as those of "the Rhinosses or Elephant Master, being a very large Creature of a Dark Colour having a long Strong horn growing upon his Nose (with which he kills Elephants)."[13]

The best-known Indian agent in Pittsburgh during the Seven Years' War was George Croghan, an Irishman who had fled his country during the 1741 potato famine and ended up in western Pennsylvania. Croghan amassed a great deal of Indian knowledge as a fur trader, and he put that information to good use when he became England's deputy superintendent of Indian affairs for the northern colonies in 1756. Among Croghan's acquaintances in England was Peter Collinson, a draper who was interested in American natural history. Collinson referred to Croghan in his June 1762 request to Philadelphia botanist John Bartram for more details about the animal remains at Big Bone Lick:

> Their Bones or skeletons are now standing in a Licking place not far from the Ohio of which I have Two of their Teeth One Greenwood an Indian Trader & my friend Geo:Croghan both saw them & gave Mee relation of them but they omitted to Take Notice what Hoofs they had, & what Horns, these two Material Articles known, would help to determine their Genus or Species—prethee inquire after them, for they are wonderful beyond description if what is related of them may be depended on.[14]

Croghan's presence at the Lick was mentioned again a few weeks later in a July letter from Collinson to Bartram that also made reference to Philadelphia publisher and inventor Benjamin Franklin:

> I forgett if I ever Mention'd two Monstrous Teeth I had sent Mee by the Govr of Virginia one tooth Weighs 3¾ pds 15 Inches round The other 1¾ pound—13½ inches round One other has Docr Fothergill & T. Pen another One Greenwood, well known to B. Franklin an Indian

Trader knocked some of the Teeth out of their Jaws, & Geo:Croghan has been att the Licking Place near the Ohio where the skelletons of six Monstrous animals was standing as they will inform thee Croghan is well known to B:Franklin To Him I wrote a Long Letter which I have Desir'd B:Franklin to show thee before He sends it to Crogan of which thou Take a Coppy if thou thinks worthwhile.[15]

Although there is no surviving copy of the communication from Collinson to Croghan via Franklin, one can guess as to its content. Collinson probably asked for details about the skeletons Croghan had observed standing at the Lick, and he likely urged Croghan to collect more bones to help identify the species to which they belonged.

Bartram, in a reply to Collinson's July letter, made no mention of having seen Collinson's correspondence to Croghan. Instead, Bartram informed Collinson that the skeletons at Big Bone Lick could not be in an upright position: "thee seems to think ye skeletons stand in ye posture ye beasts stood in when Alive which is impossible [since] ye ligaments would rot & ye bones fall out of Joints & tumble confusedly on ye ground."[16]

In a December 1762 letter to Bartram, Collinson reported that he now had three of the Lick's "Monstrous Teeth," none of which resembled the elephant molars displayed at the British Museum. The puzzling molars caused Collinson to surmise that the Lick's teeth and bones were those of "an unknown Creature—unless it may be the Rhinoceras whose teeth I have not Seen." In Bartram's May 1763 reply, he agreed with Collinson's opinion that the remains belonged to an unknown animal. He dismissed the possibility of the bones being those of rhinoceroses, since "its as difficult to account for thair comeing there as ye Elephant & ye bones [are] as much too large for one as ye other." Bartram ended by announcing his own tentative plan to obtain remains from the Lick: "if I should go there & have A proper opertunity to observe them I believe I should want A many bones to make up an intire skeleton."[17]

Although Bartram never journeyed to Big Bone Lick, Croghan returned after the conclusion of the Seven Years' War. In 1765, British authorities sent Croghan down the Ohio River to negotiate peace with the Illinois Indian tribes that were still allied with the French. Croghan left Pittsburgh on May 15, leading a party that included his personal servants, an Indian-trader cousin, a doctor friend, boatmen, and Indian deputies. The party's two bateaux (flatboats) also carried a large amount of merchandise to be given to the Illinois tribes. During the trip downriver, Croghan's men deported several Frenchmen who had been trading in Shawnee villages. On May 31, according to Croghan's journal, the party briefly left the river to visit "the great Lick, where those bones are only found, about four miles from the river." On their way to the Lick "through a fine timbered clear wood," Croghan and his men "came into a large road which the buffaloes have beaten, spacious enough for two wagons to go abreast." They followed the bison road to the Lick and collected some fossils, including a tusk more than six feet long. They discovered the remains in a bank of the Lick's creek, where stream erosion had exposed a large number of bones that had been buried five to six feet underground.

All the specimens from the Lick were lost a week later when eighty Kickapoo and Mascoutin Indians attacked Croghan's party near the mouth of the Wabash River, at the edge of Illinois country. The warriors killed five men and injured several more, including Croghan, who was tomahawked in the head. The merchandise in the boats was plundered, and the survivors were taken prisoner and marched inland to the warriors' village near the present site of Lafayette, Indiana. Croghan was able to negotiate their release when their captors became fearful of retaliatory attacks by British-friendly Ohio tribes. Croghan eventually made his way home to Philadelphia, following a circuitous route.[18]

In 1766, British authorities instructed Croghan to return to Illinois country and convince the French-leaning Indians to accept British oversight. This time, Croghan's expedition left Pittsburgh on June 18 in a flotilla of thirteen bateaux, two of which were heavily laden with provisions, trade goods, and gifts for the Indians. Croghan's large party consisted of boatmen, Indians, personal friends, military officers, and George Morgan, the junior partner of a Philadelphia trading firm. Croghan's trip log, if he kept one, did not survive. However, a journal written by Captain Harry Gordon, one of the military escorts, contains significant details about the voyage. The expedition reached the vicinity of Big Bone Lick on July 16, and an entry in Gordon's journal recalls the visit:

The 16th We encamped opposite the great Lick, and next Day I went with a Party of Indians and Batteau-Men to view this much talked of Place. the beaten Roads from all Quarters to it easily conducted Us; they resemble those to an Inland Village where Cattle go to and fro a large Common. The Pasturage near it seems of the finest kind, mixed with Grass and Herbage, and well watered; on our Arrival at the Lick which is 5 Miles distance South of the River, we discovered laying about many large Bones, some of which the exact Patterns of Elephants Tusks, & others of different parts of a large Animal. The extent of the Muddy part of the Lick is ¾ of an Acre; this Mud being of a salt quality is greedily lick'd by Buffalo, Elk & Deer, who came from distant parts, in great Numbers for this Purpose; we picked up several of the Bones, some out of ye Mud, others off the firm Ground.[19]

By the time the expedition resumed its downriver journey on July 18, Croghan and Morgan had each amassed a large collection of skeletal remains from the Lick. They transported the bones, tusks, and teeth with them to Illinois, and from there, they took the fossils by boat to New Orleans and then by ship to the East Coast. Upon returning home to Philadelphia, Morgan gave his collection to his brother John, a physician with an interest in natural history. The fossils remained in Dr. Morgan's possession until 1788, when he sold them to Dutch anatomist Petrus Camper. Croghan immediately dispatched his specimens to England, where their arrival in 1767 ignited much interest and many debates over the identity of the remains.[20]

Chapter 5

———— ❧ ————

Animal Incognitum

From all these observations I was convinced that the
grinder tooth, brought from the Ohio, was not that of
an elephant; but of some carnivorous animal, larger
than an ordinary elephant: and I could not doubt that
the tusk belonged to the same animal.
—William Hunter, 1768

The New Orleans ship carrying George Croghan and his boxes
of fossils from Big Bone Lick arrived in New York's harbor on
January 10, 1767. The onlookers who viewed the uncrated specimens agreed with Croghan's identification: the fossils were elephant remains. One observer suggested that an investigation
be made of the elephants' migration route to the Lick from Asia,
since such a study might reveal a commercially important land
passage between North America and the Orient.[1]

Six days after his arrival in New York, Croghan penned a
letter to the Earl of Shelburne, the British official in charge of
the American colonies. The letter to London announced the
completion of Croghan's written report on his western tour, and
it ended with a brief description of his visit to Big Bone Lick:
"In my passage down the River Ohio, I went to the Place, where
the Indians had often told me, There were some extraordinary
Bones. I immediately discovered, They were those of Ele-

phants." Croghan continued, "I beg leave to acquaint your Lordship, That by the first Ship from hence to London, I shall do myself the Honor, of sending your Lordship, a Box containing some Tusks, Grinders, &c." The box sent to Lord Shelburne contained two tusks, several loose molars ("grinders"), and a lower jaw with two intact molars. Croghan likely sent Shelburne the fossils in the hope that he would look favorably on Croghan's proposal to establish a British colony in Illinois.[2]

Benjamin Franklin, then a temporary resident of London, was serving as the on-site lobbyist for Croghan's Illinois colonization plan. Knowing of Franklin's interest in all things scientific, Croghan sent his friend eight fossils from Big Bone Lick: four tusks, three molars, and a vertebra. In Franklin's August 1767 letter to Croghan, he acknowledged the receipt of the specimens and noted that, strangely, the elephant molars appeared to be those of a meat-eating animal:

> I return you many thanks for the box of elephants' tusks and grinders. They are extremely curious on many accounts. . . . The tusks agree with those of the African and Asiatic elephant in being nearly of the same form and texture, and some of them, notwithstanding the length of time they just have lain, being still good ivory. But the grinders differ, being full of Knobs, like the grinders of a carnivorous animal; when those of the elephant, who eats only vegetables, are almost smooth. But then we know of no other animal with tusks like an elephant, to whom such grinders might belong.

Franklin continued his letter with the observation, "It is remarkable, that elephants now inhabit naturally only hot countries where there is no winter, and yet these remains are found in a winter country." He also noted that large numbers of elephant tusks were being found in Siberia, a region with a climate even colder than that of the Big Bone Lick area. To Franklin, it appeared "as if the earth had anciently been in another position, and the climates differently placed from what they are at present."[3]

Croghan's shipment of Big Bone Lick specimens to London proved to be a boon for Peter Collinson, who had already studied molars from the Lick. Collinson's September 1767 letter to John Bartram reflected his excitement over the "Elephant's Teeth &c., sent over to Lord Shelburn & our Frd Benj Franklin." Collinson described the remains as those of "Vast Creatures with the long Teeth or Tusks of Elephants, but with Great Grinders belonging to some animal not yett known," thereby affording "room for Endless reflection & Admiration."[4]

Collinson shared his reflections on the Lick's "vast creature" at the November 26 meeting of London's Royal Society, a century-old organization devoted to the scientific study of natural history. With a selection of Croghan's fossils laid out before the audience, Collinson showed that the unknown animal's ivory tusks clearly were elephant-like, but the pronged molars clearly were not. Anticipating the rejoinder that the tusks and molars could be the remains of two different species, Collinson reported, "no grinding teeth of elephants, are discovered with these tusks"; only "great numbers of very large pronged teeth" had been found. In the remainder of his talk, Collinson presented his objections to the theory that the unknown species at Big Bone Lick was some variety of elephant. He pointed out that Europeans had never seen living elephants in the New World, and there was "no probability of their having been brought from Africa, or Asia." Furthermore, "it is impossible that elephants could inhabit the country where these bones and teeth are now found, by reason of the severity of the winters." Collinson also rejected the idea that the fossils found at Big Bone Lick were those of tropical elephants that had drowned in Noah's Flood. That hypothesis had recently been constructed to explain the presence of elephantine remains in Siberia, which lies north of the geographic range of elephants in Asia. According to the Flood scenario, the floating carcasses of drowned elephants "were driven to the Northward, and, at the subsiding of the waters, deposited where they are now found." Collinson argued that since elephants had never occupied any of the lands south of the Ohio Valley, the biblical deluge could not have carried elephant bodies northward to Big Bone Lick.[5]

Collinson made a second presentation to the Royal Society on December 10. That lecture was concerned primarily with the pronged molars, which Collinson characterized as the teeth of a plant-eating goliath: "the animal to which these grinding teeth belong, by their make and form, seemed designed for the biting and breaking off the branches of trees and shrubs for its sustenance." Collinson's evidence for the animal's herbivorous nature came "from analogy, that the great heavy unwieldy animals, such as elephants, and the rhinoceros, &c. are not carnivorous, being unable, from want of agility and swiftness, to pursue their prey, so are wholly confined to vegetable food; and for the same reason, this great creature, to which these teeth belong, wherever it exists, is probably supported by browsing on trees and shrubs, and other vegetable food."[6]

Benjamin Franklin was evidently influenced by Collinson's two Royal Society presentations, essentially repeating parts of them in a January 31, 1768, letter to French scientist Abbé Chappe. As mentioned earlier, Franklin had previously written to Croghan that the molars from Big Bone Lick were like those of a carnivorous animal. But in his letter to Chappe, Franklin amended those initial observations, writing that the knobby teeth "might be as useful to grind the small branches of Trees, as to chaw Flesh." Franklin also sent Chappe one of the molars he had received from Croghan.[7]

Franklin's gift to Chappe was not the first Big Bone Lick molar to be shipped from England to France. Collinson had previously forwarded molars from the Lick (figure 12) to Georges-

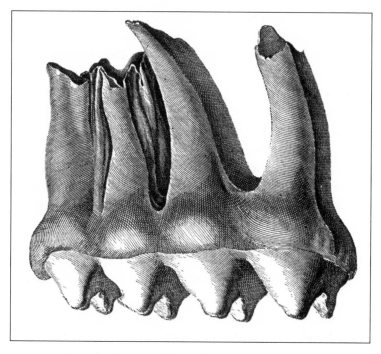

Figure 12. Molar from Big Bone Lick sent to Georges-Louis Leclerc de Buffon by Peter Collinson. (Georges-Louis Leclerc de Buffon, *The Epochs of Nature* [1778], plate 4)

Louis Leclerc de Buffon, France's leading naturalist. In a 1767 letter that accompanied the teeth, Collinson argued that all of the Lick's fossils were derived from a single species—and that species was not an elephant. In reference to Buffon's 1764 statement that the remains at Big Bone Lick were commingled fossils consisting of hippopotamus teeth and elephant tusks and bones, Collinson's letter asked, "May we not suppose that there existed formerly a large animal with the tusks of the elephant and the grinders of the hippopotamus?"[8]

Collinson personally believed that extinction was not possible because, as he explained to Bartram, "it is contrary to the common Course of Providence to suffer any of his Creatures to be Annihilated." He probably mentioned the possibility of an animal's former existence only because he knew of Buffon's interest in vanished species. In fact, Collinson's rejection of extinction was evident by his use of the present tense in his December 10, 1767, speech to the Royal Society: "this great creature, to which these teeth belong, wherever it exists, is probably supported by browsing."[9]

The Big Bone Lick fossils were the focus of yet another presentation to the Royal Society on February 25, 1768, given by Dr. William Hunter. A physician to the queen and a renowned anatomist, Hunter opened his talk by explaining how he had pursued his professional interest in the skeletal elements from Big Bone Lick. He had examined the Lick's specimens housed in London, as well as the bones and teeth of elephants, hippopotamuses, and other large animals that were held in the city's museums. Like Collinson, Hunter concluded that all of the Lick's fossils originated from a single species, "a *pseudelephant*, or *animal incognitum*, which naturalists were unacquainted with." He suspected "that this *animal incognitum* would prove to be the supposed elephant of Siberia, and other parts of Europe; and that the real elephant would be found to have been in all ages a native of Asia and Africa only." Hunter disagreed with two of Collinson's beliefs about the unknown animal, however: that it was an herbivore, and that it was still alive. Hunter argued that the molars of the *incognitum* were those of a carnivore, due to the prongs and the enamel coating on the teeth. He also thought that the species had likely vanished, perhaps due to God's benevolence: "And if this animal was indeed carnivorous, which I believe cannot be doubted, although we may as philosophers regret it, as men we cannot but thank Heaven that its whole generation is probably extinct."[10]

Three decades after the initial collection of the Lick's fossils in 1739, many questions still swirled around their identification.

Did they represent the skeletal elements of one species or two? If only one type of animal had contributed the fossils, was it the same one found in Siberia? Was the animal a geographic variety of the elephant, or was it some unknown elephant-like species? Was it herbivorous or carnivorous? Was it extant or extinct? If extant, where was it now located? If extinct, what had caused its extinction? Through the remainder of the eighteenth century, naturalists argued over these questions, while travelers continued to stop at Big Bone Lick and record and collect what they found there.

British army engineer Thomas Hutchins made his second visit to the Lick in 1768, having been there in 1766 as a member of Croghan's party. In his journal, Hutchins described the principal site yielding elephants' bones as being "of circular form, composed of a species of Quick Sand and Black Mud which is of a very Miry Quality." Hutchins expanded on Bossu's stuck-in-the-mud explanation for the bones: "It however seems not improbable, but that the whole which were in this Country (by what means soever they were brought) kept constantly in one Herd and that arriving at the Licks in a wet season, and entering to satisfy their natural thirst for the salt water which arrises from them, some of them might by their great weight have sunk so deep as not to be able to rise out & the others out of sympathy, or some other cause, not being willing to leave their companions in distress, have shared the same fate."[11]

Frontier explorer Daniel Boone, while traveling alone along the southern bank of the Ohio River in 1770, stopped by the Lick and examined its fossil remains. The site was later visited by a number of groups from the seaboard colonies. For example, a crew of easterners was guided to the location in 1773 by a band of Delaware Indians. Robert McAfee, one of the party members, described the Lick as "about 200 yards long and as wide, and the waters and mud are of a sulphur smell." McAfee added that it was "a wonder to see the large bones that lie there, which have been of several large big creatures." The group used long rib bones for tent poles and huge vertebrae for camp stools. A tusk embedded in the ground, with six feet of it extending perpendicularly above the surface, was so firmly anchored that six men could not budge it.[12]

In 1774, a company of men completed the first survey of "the large Buffalos Lick & Salt Spring known by the name of the big Bone Lick." Surveyor Thomas Hanson made special note of the remains at the site, "which the People imagined to be Elephants." Hanson recorded the presence of a broken tusk exceeding seven feet in length, with a diameter of nine inches at one end and five inches at the other.[13]

In 1775, while returning upriver to Pittsburgh, a party of surveyors, land seekers, and military men stopped at the Lick to procure some meat. The ethnicity of the group members reflected the diversity of people being drawn to the western frontier: "two Englishmen, two Irishmen, one Welshman, two Dutchmen, two Virginians, two Marylanders, one Swede, one African Negro, and a Mulatto." This census was included in the journal of British land-seeker Nicholas Cresswell (see chapter 3). Another of Cresswell's journal entries concerned the appearance of the Lick, which had been flooded by runoff from the previous night's rainstorm: "Where the bones are found is a large muddy pond, a little more than knee deep with a Salt spring in it which I suppose preserves the bones sound." The entire party stripped and entered the water in a successful search for teeth. Based on their structure, Cresswell decided that the teeth had come from "Grasseaters." He also conjectured that the Lick's large remains were those of elephants, since he found "a part of a tusk, about two feet long, Ivory to all appearance, but by length of time had grown yellow and very soft." Cresswell referred to the site as "Elephant Bone Lick," noting that the skeletal pieces were similar to those taken from Africa. Like many visitors to the Lick, Cresswell was puzzled by the presence of elephantine fossils at the site: "There neither is or ever was any Elephants in North or South America, that I can learn, or any quadruped one tenth part as large as these."[14]

The label "Big Bones" appeared at the location of the Lick on a 1778 map of the Ohio Valley drawn by Thomas Hutchins. The British army engineer also published a topographic description that included an explanation for the omission of any reference to elephants: "About 584 miles below *Fort Pitt*, and on the eastern side of the *Ohio* River, about three miles from it, at the head of a small Creek or Run, where are several large and miry Salt Springs, are found numbers of large bones, teeth and tusks, commonly supposed to be those of Elephants:—but the celebrated Doctor *Hunter* of London, in his ingenious and curious Observations on these bones, &c. has supposed them to belong to some Carnivorous animal, larger than an ordinary Elephant."[15]

William Hunter's claim that the Lick's animal was a carnivorous *incognitum* had been popularized in British books such as Thomas Pennant's *Synopsis of Quadrupeds* (1771) and Oliver Goldsmith's *An History of the Earth and Animated Nature* (1774). Neither of these works subscribed to Hunter's belief that the *incognitum* was extinct, however, since that would imply a lack of foresight on God's part. Pennant's dismissal of extinction caused him to write that the *incognitum* probably survived "in some of those remote parts of the vast new continent, unpenetrated yet by *Europeans*." According to Pennant, "Providence maintains and continues every created species." Goldsmith likewise believed that the *incognitum* was still alive but stated, "as yet this formidable creature has evaded our search."[16]

In 1777, eminent Dutch anatomist Petrus Camper, an emeritus professor of Groningen University, wrote an article in which he reviewed the Lick's fossils and questioned some of the conclusions drawn by other European investigators. He rejected the carnivore theory of his British counterpart Hunter, from

Figure 13. French naturalist Georges-Louis
Leclerc de Buffon. (A. Mary F. Robinson, *The
French Ideal* [1911], 241)

whom he had received correspondence and *incognitum* remains.
Camper also disagreed with Buffon's identification of the Big
Bone Lick molars as those of a hippopotamus; he showed that
the teeth of the unknown animal were more like those of an
elephant and that the creature probably possessed tusks and a
trunk.[17]

In 1778, Buffon (figure 13) wrote his best-known work, *Epochs of Nature*, in which he reiterated that the skeletal elements
found at Big Bone Lick were mostly hippopotamus teeth mixed
with elephant remains. However, Buffon also announced the
presence of a third organism, "an ancient species, which must be
regarded as the first and largest of terrestrial animals." Based on
the "enormous" molar that Collinson had sent to him, Buffon

concluded that although the tooth was similar to that of a hippopotamus, it had come from a creature that was extinct, "for an animal, whose species was larger than that of an elephant, could hide himself in no part of the earth so as to remain unknown."[18]

Thus, the identification of the site's specimens was still in dispute in 1780, when bones identical to those at the Lick were discovered 600 miles east in the Hudson River Valley. To follow the search for the identity of the Lick's fossils, we must now detour to New York before returning to Kentucky.

Chapter 6

—— ∽ ——

Thomas Jefferson Takes an Interest

They all take these Bones to belong to Quadrupeds. I suppose them to be human—like the Bones & Teeth at Clavarack.

—Ezra Stiles, 1781

In the autumn of 1780, a ditchdigger on the Reverend Robert Annan's New York farm unearthed four molars and some soft, decayed bones of a large animal. Annan took the teeth home and later returned with a neighbor to dig up more remains. In an account of the discovery sent to the American Academy of Arts and Sciences, Annan described the grinding surface of the huge teeth as covered by "protuberances, rising in a pyramidical form, the perpendicular height of the highest of which was about an inch and one tenth." Based on the configuration of its large molars, he surmised that the animal "had been of the carniverous kind." Annan conjectured that the unknown creature was "not a marine monster, for it lay above a hundred miles from the sea: unless we can suppose, that not many centuries ago, that part of the country was covered by the sea." As for identifying what terrestrial species it might be, the proportions of the bones argued against the animal being an elephant: "A gentleman who came to see the remains of it, told me, he had seen the skeleton of an elephant; but the biggest joint on it was much inferior to what I have described as the loin joint." Annan, a country parson, believed that the biblical Flood had probably caused the extinction of the enormous beast, whatever its identity.[1]

Annan's property was located about fifteen miles west of the Hudson River and seventy miles north of New York City, which in late 1780 was held by British troops fighting against the Continental army in the American Revolution. The Continental army, led by General George Washington, had its winter encampment in the area north of West Point, just a few miles from Annan's farm. When Washington heard about the fossils collected at the farm, he took his aide-de-camp Colonel David Humphreys and a few other officers on a December sleigh ride to view the specimens. Annan's account of his discovery made brief mention of Washington's visit: "His Excellency, General Washington, came to my house to see these relicts. He told me, he had in his house a grinder which was found on the Ohio, much resembling these." In Humphreys's description of the visit to Annan's home, he recounted that Washington had told the story of a man who had observed the extraction of molars from an *incognitum* skull at Big Bone Lick: "when they raised up the Head out of which they took the Teeth, . . . it reached up to the middle of his Face."[2]

Washington correctly discerned the similarity between the fossil molars from Annan's farm and those from the Lick. Annan's descriptions of his specimens leave no doubt that he had unearthed skeletal elements of the Lick's *incognitum* in the Hudson River Valley. Even more interesting is the fact that *incognitum* fossils had been found in the Hudson Valley seventy-five years earlier, but they had erroneously been attributed to a bipedal giant rather than to a four-footed beast. In 1705, at a site near the Hudson River settlement of Claverack, about twenty-five miles south of Albany, a Dutch farmer came upon a tooth weighing nearly five pounds. Further exploration uncovered greatly decayed bones, one of which was judged to be a crumbled human femur. Some bone fragments and the tooth were obtained by the British governor of New York, Edward Hyde, who shipped them to the Royal Society in London. Hyde recounted the speculations about the tooth's origin in his letter accompanying the bones: "Some said 'twas the tooth of a human creature; others, of some beast or fish; but nobody could tell what beast or fish had such a tooth. I was of opinion it was the tooth of a giant."[3]

News of the fossils' discovery spread into New England, aided by an article in a Boston newspaper. The Reverend Edward Taylor of Massachusetts already knew of the Claverack remains when three Dutchmen visiting his home in 1706 showed him two large teeth and two pieces of bone from a giant that they estimated had been sixty or seventy feet tall. When two of the men later showed the specimens to Massachusetts governor Joseph Dudley, they explained how the giant's height had been gauged: "there is a plain discoloration of the ground, for seventy-five foot long at least, different from the earth in colour and substance, which is judged by every body that see it, to be the ruins and dust of the body that bore those teeth and bones."[4]

Taylor took a special interest in the fossils, since he was aware of a Native American legend concerning giant people. Taylor was not surprised when his visitors told him that local Indians who had come to view the large bones upbraided the settlers for previously doubting the existence of the Hudson Valley's vanished giant. According to the Indians, the giant had been "a monstrous person as high as the Tops of the Pine Trees, that would hunt Bears till they took the Trees, & then would catch them with his Hands."[5]

Upon hearing of the Claverack remains, Taylor began writing about the giant in an epic poem that he never finished. Years later, Taylor's grandson Ezra Stiles came across the poem in a collection of Taylor's unpublished poetry. The young Stiles learned of the Hudson Valley giant both from his grandfather's

Figure 14. Ezra Stiles first identified the Lick's fossils as the remains of a human giant. (Library of Congress, Prints and Photographs Division)

poem and from his uncle Eldad Taylor, who told him that, according to Native American lore, the giant was peaceful and would not hurt the Indians.[6]

Stiles's interest in the Claverack giant was piqued in 1750 when, while working as a tutor at Yale College, he saw a four-pound molar that was being taken from New York to Boston. In 1760, while employed as a pastor in Newport, Rhode Island, Stiles wrote of a gentleman from Nantucket who had acquired a "Jaw Bone of a Giant." By this time, Stiles (figure 14) was convinced that the fossil remains were those of extinct giants, since there was *"no Animal on Earth or in the Ocean* of a Magnitude adequate to these Bones and Teeth." In 1777, while serving as a minister in Portsmouth, New Hampshire, Stiles was shown a fossil molar that had likely been taken from Big Bone Lick. He concluded in his diary, "It is a Grinder Tooth of some great Animal, but whether an Elephant or Gyant, is a Question."[7]

Stiles was inaugurated as the president of Yale College in 1778, and in that capacity he hosted a June 1784 visit by Thomas Jefferson, the recently named U.S. ambassador to France. After that meeting, Jefferson wrote a letter requesting Stiles's views on the large skeletal remains being collected from Big Bone Lick and the Hudson Valley, as well as from Siberia:

> After I had the pleasure of seeing you in New Haven I received information that you were in possession of several facts relative to the huge bones of the Animal incognitum found in America, or of the Mammoth as the Russians call the same animal whose bones they also find in the Northern parts of their empire. Monsr. de Buffon, the celebrated Physiologist of the present age, . . . adopted an opinion which I think not founded in fact. It is that this animal was the same with the elephant of Asia and Africa. I think it certain that it was a different animal. Having therefore on a particular occasion drawn his opinion into question I am still anxious of getting every additional information on the subject which may serve either to confirm or to correct the conclusion I had formed. I take the liberty therefore of asking from you a communication of whatever facts you may have become acquainted with as to this animal.[8]

Stiles's reply to Jefferson recounted the Hudson Valley discoveries, including the recent find at Annan's farm. Stiles also wrote of the huge fossils found in other localities and mentioned that George Washington owned a molar from Big Bone Lick that had been "taken out of a Head which when erect reached from the Ground to a Mans Eyes. What Quadruped has such a Head[?]" The entire text of Stiles's multipage letter reflected his belief that the skeletal remains were those of extinct human goliaths. He summed up his position in a single sentence: "But I will hazard my Reputation with you, Sir, and give it as my opinion that the huge fossil Bones, Teeth and parts of Skeletons dug up in Siberia, in Germany, France and other parts of Europe, and finally those on the Ohio and elsewhere in America, appertain, *not to Quadrupeds, not to Sea-Animals, but to Bipeds* of huge and immense Stature."[9]

Jefferson wrote back to Stiles in 1785 and thanked him for the description of the large bones found in the Hudson Valley. Jefferson continued, "I suspect that these must have been of the same animal with those found on the Ohio: and if so, they could not have belonged to any human figure, because they are accompanied with tusks of the size, form and substance of those of the elephant." Jefferson related that he had seen some very good ivory from tusks collected at Big Bone Lick and guessed that the Lick's *incognitum* had been much bigger than a present-day elephant.[10]

Jefferson's logic caused Stiles to revise his opinion. For example, in his diary entry of April 26, 1786, Stiles referred to the "Elephants Teeth" from Big Bone Lick that General Samuel Parsons was giving to Yale and Harvard. Two weeks later, in a letter to Jefferson, Stiles wrote that he no longer believed that the remains were those of giants: "I was mistaken in thinking the Ohio Teeth and Bones did not belong to the Elephant." He explained that Jefferson's "learned Letter led me to reexamine the Skeleton of the Elephant in the Phil. Transactions, But what is most decisive with me is the *Tusks* found at the Ohio, which are indubitably Elephants." Stiles also agreed with Jefferson's position that the elephant found at Big Bone Lick was different from the elephant of Asia and Africa, since the Lick's fossil molars were those of a carnivorous animal.[11]

Stiles, Jefferson, and other noted Americans had become interested in the *incognitum* due to a variety of personal experiences. Stiles's fascination began with the reading of his grandfather's poem. Benjamin Franklin was enticed when his friend George Croghan presented him with specimens from Big Bone Lick. Likewise, Washington became intrigued following his acquisition of a molar from the Lick. In contrast, Jefferson's interest in the animal started when he was asked to complete a survey from the French government.

In 1780, the Marquis Francois Barbe-Marbois, secretary of the French Legation in Philadelphia, compiled questionnaires for each of the states that France was assisting in the American Revolution. Jefferson, then serving as Virginia's governor, answered the twenty-two queries directed to his state. Although he resigned from the governorship in 1781, Jefferson continued to revise and expand on his answers, eventually generating a book manuscript entitled *Notes from the State of Virginia*. He had 200 copies of the tome printed for private distribution in 1785, and in 1787, 1,000 additional copies were printed for public sale.[12]

Jefferson's *Notes* addressed the French inquiries in the order they were asked. The sixth query requested information about the minerals and organisms of Virginia, which then included the lands of West Virginia and Kentucky. The first animal mentioned in Jefferson's answer was the state's largest species, "the Mammoth, or big buffalo, as called by the Indians." He wrote that the mammoth had vanished from the East but might still survive in remote American regions unaffected by the Indians' trading of animal skins for European goods:

Such is the economy of nature, that no instance can be produced of her having permitted any one race of her animals to become extinct; of her having formed any link in her great work so weak as to be broken. To add to this, the traditionary testimony of the Indians [is] that this animal still exists in the northern and western parts of America. . . . Those parts still remain in their aboriginal state, unexplored and undisturbed by us, or by others for us. He may as well exist there now, as he did formerly where we find his bones. If he be a carnivorous animal, as some Anatomists have conjectured, and the Indians affirm, his early retirement may be accounted for from the general destruction of the wild game by the Indians, which commences in the first instant of their connection with us, for the purpose of purchasing matchcoats, hatchets, and fire locks, with their skins.[13]

Thus, Jefferson entertained the notion that the mammoth was a carnivore and spurned the possibility that the mammoth, or any other species, was extinct. He also dismissed the conjecture that the remains found at Big Bone Lick were teeth of the hippopotamus mixed with tusks and bones of the elephant:

It is remarkable that the tusks and skeletons have been ascribed by the naturalists of Europe to the elephant, while the grinders have been given to the hippopotamus, or riverhorse. Yet it is acknowledged, that the tusks and skeletons are much larger than those of the elephant, and the grinders many times greater than those of the hippopotamus, and essentially different in form. Wherever these grinders are found, there also we find the tusks and skeleton; but no skeleton of the hippopotamus nor grinders of the elephant. It will not be said that the hippopotamus and elephant came always to the same spot, the former to deposit his grinders, and the latter his tusks and skeleton. For what became of the parts not deposited there? We must agree then that these remains belong to each other, that they are of one and the same animal, that this was not a hippopotamus, because the hippopotamus had no tusks nor such a frame, and because the grinders differ in their size as well as in the number and form of their points. That it was not an elephant, I think ascertained by proofs equally decisive.[14]

Jefferson's proof that the Lick's animal was not an elephant included the facts that its bones were larger, its molar surfaces were bumpy, and its geographic range was situated well north of the tropics. Jefferson rejected Buffon's speculation that the northern latitudes had once been warm enough to support elephants. He found it simpler to believe that the mammoth was not a member of the tropical elephant species but was instead a cold-adapted, elephant-like animal with a circumpolar distribution.

Finally, Jefferson employed the mammoth to counter another of Buffon's ideas: the theory of American degeneracy. That theory stated that animal species degenerated in the New World because its soils and climates were inferior to those of the Old World. Buffon's theory, which reflected Europe's sense of superiority over its American colonies, included four claims: (1) there were fewer species in the New World, (2) the species unique to the New World were smaller on average, (3) the domesticated species brought to the New World degenerated in size, and (4) the species common to both the Old and New Worlds (including humans) were smaller in the New World.

Jefferson marshaled evidence in his book to refute each of Buffon's four contentions. For example, Jefferson presented data showing that New World individuals weighed at least as much as Old World individuals of the same circumpolar species, including the polar bear, moose, beaver, otter, and lynx. Jefferson also pointed out that the size equivalence was true even for the world's largest terrestrial animal: "The bones of the Mammoth which have been found in America, are as large as those found in the old world." According to Jefferson, the very existence of the mammoth in the New World "should have sufficed to have rescued the earth it inhabited, and the atmosphere it breathed, from the imputation of impotence in the conception and nourishment of animal life on a large scale: to have stifled, in its birth, the opinion of a writer, the most learned too of all others in the science of animal history, that . . . nature is less active, less energetic on one side of the globe than she is on the other."[15]

Americans eagerly embraced Jefferson's refutation of Buffon's theory, and the mammoth quickly became a symbol of the strength of the young country and its parity with the Old World. In contrast to the European nations that perceived their cultural legacy in the classical ruins of Greece and Rome, American nationalism soon came to be expressed by the relics of the mammoth in the New World's unspoiled landscape. Paul Semonin's recent book *American Monster* thoroughly covers the evolution of the mammoth into an early icon of American patriotism.[16]

While Jefferson (figure 15) was working on his growing manuscript during the early 1780s, the apparent importance of the mammoth led him to seek more knowledge about the animal. In December 1781, he gave Daniel Boone a letter to convey to the Louisville home of General George Rogers Clark, commander of the Army of the West, which was then engaged in battling Indians on the frontier. Clark shared Jefferson's interest in the natural world and apparently had promised to send Jefferson some fossil remains from Big Bone Lick. The purpose of Jefferson's letter was to remind Clark of his offer and to request different types of teeth: "Were it possible to get a tooth of each kind, that is to say a foretooth, grinder &c. it would particularly oblige me."[17]

Clark's February 1782 reply stated that he was "unhappy that it hath been out of my power to procure you those Curiosities you want except a large thigh Bone that dont please me being broke." Clark assured Jefferson that his soldiers would visit the Lick in the coming months to collect teeth and other skeletal

Figure 15. Thomas Jefferson encouraged fossil collecting at Big Bone Lick from 1781 to 1807. (Library of Congress, Prints and Photographs Division)

materials: "I shall have the largest and fairest got—a Thigh and Jaw Bone Grinders and Tusk. The Animal had no foreteeth that I could ever discover and by no means Carnivorous as many suppose."[18]

It seems that Jefferson had not yet received any remains from the Lick when he next wrote to Clark. In a November 1782 letter mailed from Richmond, Jefferson restated his great interest in the fossils: "A specimen of each of the several species of bones now to be found is to me the most desireable object in Natural history, and there is no expense of package or of safe transportation which I will not gladly reimburse to procure them safely." Not trusting that this letter would reach Clark, Jefferson wrote a follow-up letter from Philadelphia in which he repeated his request for fossils of the "big buffalo," the Indian name for the mammoth.[19]

Clark's October 1783 reply echoed his previous apology: "I am sorry it hath not been in my power to procure the Bones that I promised you. The situation of the place whare they are found is such that a small party dare not venture in time of war, being nearer to s[ai]d Enemy than to our own settlements." Clark noted that when several soldiers had hunted game at the Lick the previous winter, they reported that the fossil pieces lying on the surface had all been carried away, and the remaining bones were buried in soil "so frozen that it was impossible they could get them having nothing to dig with but their small Tomahawks." Clark pledged that Jefferson would receive the requested fossils within the next year because, with the recent defeat of the region's Indians, they could now be safely collected.[20]

In Jefferson's December 1783 acknowledgment of Clark's reply, he thanked him for being "so kind as to keep alive the hope of getting for me as many of the different species of bones, teeth and tusks of the *Mammoth* as can now be found." Jefferson also asked Clark whether he would be interested in leading an expedition to investigate the natural features between the Mississippi River and the Pacific Ocean. Clark's February 1784 response again promised to procure Big Bone Lick fossils for Jefferson: "The Bones you wish for will undoubtedly be sent to you without some misfortune should happen to me." Clark also expressed his willingness to lead a western tour, assuming that the necessary monies could be raised. Unfortunately, Jefferson's two-decade delay in arranging the trip meant that Clark was too old to command the strenuous expedition, which was led instead by Meriwether Lewis and William Clark, the youngest brother of George Rogers Clark.[21]

It is unknown whether Jefferson ever received any Big Bone Lick fossils from Clark. An entry in Stiles's diary recapitulated his June 1784 conversation with Jefferson that had touched on the topic of remains from the Lick: "Gov. Jefferson has seen many of the great Bones dug up on the Ohio. He has a thighbone *Three Feet long*—& a Tooth weighing *sixteen Pounds*." The tooth to which Stiles referred, however, may not have been collected at the Lick; it may have been a molar sent to Jefferson in 1782 from a salt spring in the Virginia mountains. The femur may not have come from the Lick either, since by then, remains of the *incognitum* were being unearthed at many locations in eastern North America.[22]

Chapter 7

Chapter 7

A Question of Tusks

It appears somewhat extraordinary, at the first view, that
we should discover manifest proofs of there having existed
animals of which we can form no adequate idea, and which
in size must have far exceeded any thing now known upon
the earth; and those signs too, in climates where the elephant (the largest animal now in existence) is never
found.
—Gilbert Imlay, 1792

Thomas Jefferson's desire to acquire Big Bone Lick fossils was
matched by that of Dr. Christian Friedrich Michaelis. The German doctor had come to America in 1779 to serve as a physician
for Hessian troops fighting alongside the British in the American Revolution. Dr. Michaelis's father, a University of Göttin-
gen professor, was aware of the Big Bone Lick fossils that had
been sent to Europe and probably urged his son to collect remains of the *incognitum* during his stay in America.

While in New York, Michaelis learned of the fossils that had
been discovered on the Reverend Annan's farm and likely heard
about George Washington's interest in the *incognitum*. At the end
of the war in 1782, he requested Washington's assistance in uncovering additional remains on Annan's property. Washington
provided a dozen men and the necessary equipment for a fossil

dig that proved to be unsuccessful. Michaelis departed the farm with only a few specimens that Annan had discovered previously.[1]

By 1783, Michaelis had moved on to Philadelphia, where he made plans to take a collecting trip to Big Bone Lick. He gathered information from Thomas Hutchins and George Morgan, both past visitors to the Lick. But he also learned that a journey to the site was not recommended, due to the frequent Indian attacks taking place in the Ohio Valley. Although Michaelis was again frustrated in his quest for *incognitum* remains, while in Philadelphia he was able to arrange for drawings to be made of the Big Bone Lick fossils collected by George Morgan and currently in the possession of his brother, Dr. John Morgan. Michaelis commissioned artist Charles Willson Peale to draw life-size illustrations of each piece, and the specimens were temporarily moved to his studio. Visitors' admiration for the fossils persuaded Peale to establish his American Museum, a forerunner to the Smithsonian Institution.[2]

Michaelis returned to Germany by way of England, where he stopped to examine Big Bone Lick fossils in London collections. Once at home, he corresponded with Petrus Camper and other European anatomists before summarizing his findings in a 1789 publication. Michaelis concluded that the bones and teeth were those of an herbivorous animal; he also suggested that it was the same species as the Siberian mammoth and was probably extinct. Michaelis pointed to the knobby molars as proof that the animal was not simply a geographic race of elephant. Also, according to Michaelis, the vanished species lacked the tusks and trunk of an elephant. This remarkable conclusion resulted from his erroneous interpretation of Peale's drawing of an upper jawbone's posterior fragment (figure 16). Michaelis mistakenly thought that the illustration depicted the anterior portion, so he concluded that there was no space available for tusks or a trunk.

Michaelis's error greatly influenced Camper, who, after ex-

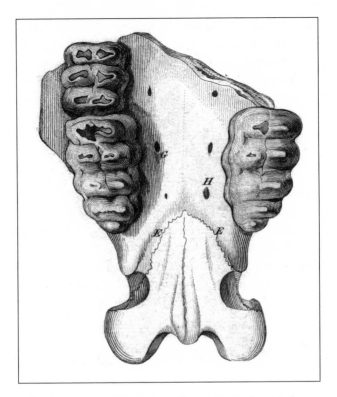

Figure 16. Posterior fragment of an upper jawbone collected at Big Bone Lick. (Drawing by Charles Willson Peale, reproduced in Georges Cuvier, *Recherches sur les ossemens fossiles*, 3rd ed. [1825], vol. 1, p. 248, plate 2)

amining an upper jawbone at the British Museum and a copy of Peale's drawing, withdrew his previous hypothesis that the *incognitum* had possessed tusks and a trunk. Camper now believed that "the animal never had tusks, and that the tusks found intermixed with the bones of the incognitum belonged most certainly to Elephants." This incorrect interpretation of Peale's drawing and a museum specimen not only precluded the existence of elephant features on the head of the *incognitum* but also lent support to reports that the tusks and other remains scattered about the Lick originated from elephants rather than from some unknown species.[3]

John Filson may have been the first non-Indian visitor to Big Bone Lick who did not believe that the Lick's fossils came from elephants. Filson was a well-educated man who had worked as a schoolteacher in Delaware prior to becoming a frontier surveyor and land speculator in the 1780s. Among his many land claims was a 5,000-acre parcel approximately ten miles from the Lick. Filson published a map of Kentucky in 1784, where the Lick's location on Big Bone Creek was identified by three labels: "Salt Springs," "a Medicinal Spring," and "the large Bones are found here" (figure 17). In the map's accompanying book, *The Discovery, Settlement, and Present State of Kentucke*, Filson reported that the bones at the Lick were *similar* to those of the elephant: "There is no other terrestrial animal now known large enough to produce them. The tusks with which they are equally furnished, equally produce true ivory. These external resemblances have generally made superficial observers conclude, that they could belong to no other than that prince of quadrupeds."[4]

Filson next reviewed the major reasons why he and other learned people rejected the elephant identification and instead concluded that the remains were those of a vanished, unknown animal. He made reference to the curious shape of the teeth, the nontropical climate of Kentucky, and the absence of elephant sightings in the Americas. Filson ended the book's section on the Lick with conjecture as to why humans would have been delighted by the disappearance of the *incognitum:*

> Happy we that it has [become extinct]. How formidable an enemy to the human species, an animal as large as the elephant, and tyrant of the forests, perhaps the devourer of man! Nations, such as the Indians, must have been in perpetual alarm. The animosities among the various tribes must have been suspended till the common enemy, who

Figure 17. Detail from John Filson's 1784 *This Map of Kentucke, etc.* (Library of Congress, Geography and Map Division)

threatened the very existence of all, should be extirpated. To this circumstance we are probably indebted for a fact, which is perhaps singular in its kind, the extinction of a whole race of animals from the system of nature.[5]

Filson's book proved to be enormously popular—"the new nation's first best-seller"—so his interpretation of the Lick's fossils was widely read. However, the idea that the Lick's *incognitum* had become extinct continued to be rejected by many. For example, in a 1786 magazine article on Big Bone Lick remains collected during the 1780s by Major Isaac Craig (figure 18), the anonymous author dismissed the possibility that the fossils were relics of a vanished organism: "I believe our globe, and every part and particle thereof, came out of the hand of its creator as perfect as he intended it should be, and will continue in exactly

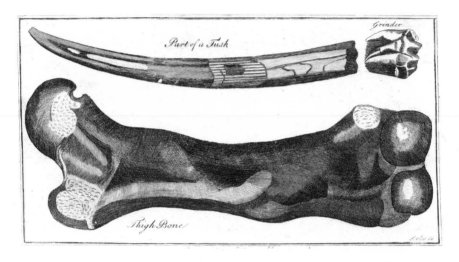

Figure 18. Tusk fragment, molar, and femur collected at Big Bone Lick by Isaac Craig. (William Winterbotham, *A Geographical, Commercial, and Philosophical View of the Present Situation of the United States of America* [1795], vol. 3, p. 138)

the same state (as to its inhabitants at least) till its final dissolution." The writer conceded that the particular animal species had become locally extinct in some places but saw no "reason to suppose any, the minutest animalcule, even inferior to those discoverable by the microscope, has been, or ever will be, annihilated, before this heaven and earth are done away."[6]

Craig was not the only soldier to collect fossils at the Lick. In 1785, Lieutenant Ebenezer Denny was part of a contingent of soldiers who traveled to the Lick from Fort Finney, a stockade located twenty miles north on the Ohio River. According to Denny's military journal, they dug up and collected "some astonishing large bones."[7]

General Samuel H. Parsons, a Revolutionary War veteran and an attorney by trade, gathered bones, tusks, and teeth from the Lick during a land surveillance trip down the Ohio River to Louisville. In a letter recounting the 1785 journey, the cautious lawyer refrained from speculating about the identity of the fossil animals, but he did express his personal view that they were extinct: "Of what species they were, by what means, and at what time, they became extinct I leave to the enquiry of Others."[8] Parsons also described his visit to Big Bone Lick in an article published by the American Academy of Arts and Sciences. He alluded to the Lick's animal being a meat eater, characterizing the Native American conception of the creature as "so fabulous, that no conjecture can be aided by it; unless it be, that the animal was a carnivorous one." Parsons described the Lick as an unforested twenty-acre area in which soft clay surrounded a stream of brackish water. He collected bones from the surface as well as from four feet or more underground. Parsons did not find an entire skeleton, but he carried away about 400 pounds of skeletal pieces.[9]

As the end of the eighteenth century approached, no one had yet collected a skeleton of the *incognitum*. The knowledge to be gained by such a discovery was highlighted in "Those Inquiries in Natural Philosophy, Which at Present Are Most Beneficial to the United States of North America," a 1789 presentation to the American Philosophical Society by Swedish Lutheran minister Nicholas Collin. In 1792, Charles Willson Peale lamented that although enormous bones of the unknown species had been found at many locations in the nation, "no tolerable idea at present can be formed of what kind of beast they were." He believed that if "a number of those bones were collected together, and made into a complete skeleton, it would lead to an illustration of the animal by analogy."[10]

In the 1790s, a natural history museum was proposed to be built in Lexington, Kentucky, with an *incognitum* skeleton from Big Bone Lick as its central exhibit. The major problem was that recovering such a skeleton would have been very difficult, since the Lick's skeletal elements were scattered throughout the site and were often broken as well. Kentuckian James Taylor, founder of Newport and a frequent visitor to the Lick in the 1790s, considered the site's dispersed and fractured remains to be evidence of the beast's carnivorous nature. He wrote that the crushed pieces undoubtedly "had been masticated by the big animals of former days whose bones were so numerously found."[11]

Late-eighteenth-century travelers who stopped at Big Bone Lick continued to collect its fossils. In 1793, the Tammany Society's museum in New York City displayed a four-pound molar taken from the Lick the previous year. The Reverend James Smith, who visited the Lick in 1795, wrote in his journal that bones were "lying round about the spring in abundance and were truly of a most enormous size. A person living at the place informed me that the bones are mostly under ground and are got by digging." Around the same time, while serving as an army captain at Fort Washington in Cincinnati, future U.S. president William Henry Harrison amassed thirteen large barrels of the Lick's remains and shipped them to Pittsburgh. The boat carrying the fossils may have sunk, since they never reached their destination.[12]

Big Bone Lick fossils were in demand in France as well. In 1796, zoologists Étienne Geoffroy Saint-Hilaire and Jean-Baptiste Lamarck of the Muséum National d'Histoire Naturelle in Paris agreed to exchange specimens with Charles Willson Peale's American Museum in Philadelphia. The French institution was especially interested in the "enormous bones which are found in great quantity on the borders of the Ohio." The Paris museum, the successor of the Jardin du Roi and its associated Cabinet du Roi, already owned several fossils from the Lick. The museum's desire to obtain additional *incognitum* remains was due to a newly inaugurated study of its elephantine specimens by Georges Cuvier (figure 19), the understudy to the chair of animal anatomy.[13]

In the course of his research on the Lick's *incognitum*, Cuvier became puzzled by Petrus Camper's statement that the ani-

Figure 19. French scientist Georges Cuvier determined that the Lick's *incognitum* was neither an elephant nor a Siberian mammoth. (Karl A. von Zittel, *History of Geology and Palaeontology* [1914], 160)

mal had been tuskless and trunkless—as noted earlier, a conclusion based on a misreading of Peale's drawing of a broken upper jawbone. Camper had died in 1789, so Cuvier sent a letter to his son Adrien, also an anatomist, requesting that he reexamine his father's interpretation of Peale's illustration. Adrien Camper initially supported his father's opinion but, after further study, wrote to Cuvier that his father had been mistaken:

"The result of my researches on the unknown animal of Ohio, is not conformable with what I formerly put forward on the subject; the piece in question is not the anterior, but the posterior fragment of the jaws."[14]

Preliminary findings from Cuvier's research were published in a 1796 article, "Memoir on the Species of Elephants, Both Living and Fossil." Dealing first with living elephants, the article announced that there were two species: Asian and African. Other biologists had suspected this, but Cuvier was able to confirm the anatomical differences between the museum's two elephant skulls—one from Ceylon (now Sri Lanka), and the other from the Cape of Good Hope in South Africa. He wrote: "It is clear that the elephant from Ceylon differs more from that of Africa than the horse from the ass or the goat from the sheep. Thus we should no longer be astonished if they do not have the same nature or the same habits."

Cuvier next considered the fossils of the Siberian mammoth and the Big Bone Lick *incognitum*. He concluded that the two extinct animals were not geographic races of a single proboscidean species but were in fact separate species, neither of which was a modern-day elephant: "The teeth and jaws of the [Siberian] mammoth do not exactly resemble those of the elephant; while as for the same parts of the Ohio animal, a glance is sufficient to see that they differ still further." Because they were not present-day elephants, Cuvier hypothesized that the two animals had been adapted to tolerate the coldness of the northern latitudes where their fossils were found. He concluded: "These animals thus differ from the elephant as much as, or more than, the dog differs from the jackal and the hyena. Since the dog tolerates the cold of the north, while the other two only live in the south, it could be the same with these animals."

Cuvier closed his paper with questions about the disappearance of the Lick's *incognitum* and the Siberian mammoth, along with five other species known solely on the basis of their fossils (a deer and a crocodile from Holland, a bear from Bavaria, a rhinoceros from Siberia, and a ground sloth from Paraguay):

> What has become of these two enormous animals of which one no longer finds any traces, and so many others of which the remains are found everywhere on earth and of which perhaps none still exist? . . .
> What was this nature that was not subject to man's dominion? And what revolution was able to wipe it out, to the point of leaving no trace of it except some half-decomposed bones? . . .
> It is not for us to involve ourselves in the vast field of conjectures that these questions open up. Only more daring philosophers undertake that.[15]

One of those "daring philosophers" was George Turner, who offered his opinions on the subject in July 1797 at the American Philosophical Society in Philadelphia. There, Turner presented his observations on Big Bone Lick fossils collected in the early 1790s, during which time he had served as a federal judge in the Ohio Valley. Turner began his paper by reviewing the scholarly activity that had followed the unearthing of enormous fossils in the northern latitudes of the Old and New Worlds: "It engaged the attention and drew forth the labours of several eminent men. Some ascribed them to the elephant; others to the hippopotamus; and others, again, to some unknown creature, larger than either, and of the carnivorous kind. To this animal incognitum common consent has given the name of Mammoth."

Turner then revealed a surprising new fact about the Lick's remains. According to Turner, the Lick contained "the remains of a second incognitum, whose stature was not, perhaps, inferior to that of the other." He observed that the "second remains evince a member of the *herbivorous* order; and, from their extraordinary size, I have no hesitation in believing, that they belonged to some link in the chain of animal creation, which, like that of the Mammoth, has long been lost." Turner reported that because the fossils of the two *incognita* were "usually embedded in company, they have hitherto been confounded together by writers, under the single appellation of Mammoth bones." The two species could be differentiated by their molars, however: "The masticating surface of the Mammoth tooth is set with four or five high double-coned processes, strongly coated with enamel; whereas that of the other *incognitum* is flat, nearly smooth, and ribbed transversely." For Turner, the contrasting molars "unquestionably bespeak the remains of two distinct species of non-descript animals; the one carnivorous, or mixed; the other herbivorous, or graminivorous."

Turner also noted the presence of two kinds of tusks, or *defenses*, as he called them. The longer defense "bears a near resemblance, in size, form and substance, to the tusk of an elephant." The shorter defense "describes a greater curve, and is so flattened or compressed on two opposite sides, in its whole length, as to produce a greater breadth than thickness, in the proportion of about two parts and a half to one." The obvious conclusion would have been that there were two types of tusks because there were two types of *incognita*. Turner, however, believed that the tusks, though differently shaped, were worn by only one of the species, the herbivorous *incognitum*. He pointed out that defensive tusks would "be incompatible with the natural pursuits" of the carnivorous mammoth.

Turner also reported on the appearance of Big Bone Lick to "furnish a corroborative presumption, if not a proof, that the Mammoth was carnivorous, or partly so." He first described the Lick's location along Big Bone Creek, with the stream cutting a channel through the site. He then presented a lengthy depiction of the Lick as the hunting ground of the leaping, ambushing mammoth:

Upon either margin of the stream there lies a stratum, extending a considerable distance, composed entirely of the bones of the buffalo and other smaller animals. . . . . From the effect of the mineral salt, these remains were in a state of high preservation—But, judge of my surprize, when attentively examining them, I discovered, that almost every bone of any length had received a fracture, occasioned, most likely, by the teeth of the Mammoth, while in the act of feeding on his prey.

It is well known that the buffalo, deer, elk and some other animals, are in the constant habit of making such places their resort; in order to drink the salt water and lick the impregnated earth. Now, may we not from these facts infer, that Nature had allotted to the Mammoth the beasts of the forest for his food? How can we otherwise account for the numerous fractures that every where mark these strata of bones? May it not be inferred, too, that as the largest and swiftest quadrupeds were appointed for his food, he necessarily was endowed with great strength and activity?—that, as the immense volume of the creature would unfit him for coursing after his prey through thickets and woods, Nature had furnished him with the power of taking it by a mighty leap?—That this power of springing to a great distance was requisite to the more effectual concealment of his bulky volume while lying in wait for prey? The Author of existence is wise and just in all his works. He never confers an appetite without the power to gratify it.

Turner concluded his paper by echoing the oft-repeated conjecture that humans were responsible for the predatory mammoth's extinction: "With the agility and ferocity of the tiger; with a body of unequalled magnitude and strength, it is possible the Mammoth may have been at once the terror of the forest and of man!—And may not the human race have made the extirpation of this terrific disturber a common cause?" Turner did not offer a reason for the extinction of the second, plant-eating *incognitum*—an animal that would become better known during the next several years as more of its remains were identified at Big Bone Lick.[16]

Chapter 8

—— ∾ ——

William Goforth's Stolen Specimens

> Filled with a strong conviction of his existence, I sought
> for evidence; I spared no labour; I dug all around, and at
> length drew from the reluctant earth the remains of a huge
> carnivorous animal, furnished with high-coned teeth,
> armed with claws.
>
> —Thomas Ashe, 1806

In his 1797 address to fellow members of the American Philosophical Society, George Turner reiterated the oft-stated need
for a "scientific description of the whole skeleton of an *incognitum* so interesting as the Mammoth." Turner declared that the
person "who shall first procure the complete skeleton of this *incognitum*, will render,—not to this country alone, but to the
world,—a most invaluable present." In 1799, the Philosophical
Society prepared and distributed a circular highlighting the importance of finding "one or more entire skeletons of the Mammoth, so called, and of such other unknown animals as either
have been, or hereafter may be discovered in America." The circular, which specifically cited Big Bone Lick as a promising site
for such a discovery, was signed by Turner and three other members who were engaged in the study of fossils: Dr. Caspar Wistar, a prominent Philadelphia physician and the nation's leading
anatomist, Charles Willson Peale, the noted artist and museum

owner, and Thomas Jefferson, the vice president of the United States and president of the American Philosophical Society.[1]

Despite the fame of Big Bone Lick as the most prolific producer of mammoth remains, the first discovery of an almost complete skeleton actually occurred just a few miles from the Reverend Annan's property in New York State. The unearthing of the skeleton began in late 1799 when workers uncovered a mammoth femur while excavating marl fertilizer from a pit on John Masten's farm. Masten, his laborers, and his neighbors then dug up more of the skeleton, laying out the bones, tusks, and teeth on the floor of Masten's granary. Their work continued for four days until water from surrounding springs filled the pit.[2]

When Jefferson heard of the discovery, he asked a friend who lived in the vicinity of Masten's farm to inquire whether the excavated pieces were for sale. Jefferson's attempt to buy the bones failed, but Peale succeeded in purchasing them in 1801. His total outlay for the bones was $200, plus a new gun for Masten's son and new gowns and other articles for Masten's wife and daughters. For an additional $100, Peale also bought the right to search the marl pit for the missing parts of the skeleton.[3] Peale first had to empty the water-filled pit, so he engaged "an ingenious mill-wright" to construct an apparatus consisting of complicated scaffolding and a twenty-foot-diameter wheel. As three or four men walked abreast inside the wheel, they activated a chain of buckets that bailed the water out of the pit and emptied it into a sixty-foot-long trough leading to a natural basin. With the assistance of a ship's pump, the elaborate machine lowered the water level to a point where workers were able to enter the pit.

A twenty-five-man crew labored several weeks to recover additional parts of the mammoth skeleton from the marl. Crowds of spectators made their way to the pit from a nearby highway and cheered the men on. According to an account by Peale's son

Rembrandt, "rich and poor, men, women, and children, all flocked to see the operation; and a swamp always noted as the solitary abode of snakes and frogs, became the active scene of curiosity and bustle." After work at the Masten farm was completed, Peale collected additional mammoth remains from marl pits at two nearby properties before returning to his Philadelphia museum.[4]

Rembrandt Peale carved wooden replicas and made papiermâché models of some of the bones. Then, with the assistance of Wistar, the elder Peale used the reproductions along with the real bones to construct two nearly complete skeletons. On both skeletons, the top of the skull and the end of the tail were missing, since those parts had not been found at any of the three collecting sites. Neither toenails nor claws had been uncovered either. The mounted skeletons measured eleven feet high at the shoulders and fifteen feet long from chin to rump. One skeleton was displayed in Peale's museum by the end of 1801, and Rembrandt and his brother Rubens took the other skeleton to England the following year.[5]

While in London during 1803, Rembrandt Peale rewrote and enlarged the pamphlet that accompanied the exhibited skeleton, adding interpretive details concerning the bones, tusks, and molars. On the basis of the teeth and other skeletal parts, he concluded that the extinct mammoth had been a carnivore but not a tuskless, leaping predator. Rather, he believed that the mammoth had been a tusked, semiaquatic animal that employed its trunk to capture fish, turtles, crustaceans, and mollusks from streams and lakes.[6] Rembrandt postulated that the mammoth's tusks had not curved upward like those of an elephant, even though his father had positioned them that way on the two reconstructed skeletons. Instead, he believed that the tusks had pointed downward like those of a walrus. He theorized that they had been employed to dislodge shellfish from the water bottom and to assist the mammoth in climbing the banks of rivers and lakes. The tusks on the two mammoth skeletons were subsequently turned downward, and that is how they remained into the 1820s.[7]

Toward the end of his 1803 narrative, Peale pointed out that three other "animals of enormous magnitude have formerly existed in America, perhaps at the same time, and of natures very opposite." The first of the other extinct species listed by Peale was the herbivorous *incognitum* represented among the remains collected from Big Bone Lick: "there have been found in Kentucky several very large *graminivorous* teeth, never known to be accompanied with any other parts (unless perhaps the tusks), and always much decayed. They appear to me exactly like those found in Siberia."[8]

The second extinct animal was the giant ground sloth whose bones had been uncovered from the floor of a West Virginia cave in 1796. Jefferson came into possession of some of the animal's bones and named the creature *megalonyx* (Greek for "great claw"); he conjectured that the animal had been a type of huge lion. When Wistar examined the remains, however, he concluded that the bones were similar to those of a present-day tree sloth and the megatherium, an extinct ground sloth from Paraguay whose skeleton had been illustrated by Georges Cuvier. The large claws of megalonyx and megatherium caused George Turner and others to speculate that the mammoth had likewise been a clawed beast.[9]

The third extinct animal tallied by Peale was the giant bison whose skull had recently been found in Kentucky. That specimen, discovered in a creek bed between twelve and fourteen miles north of Big Bone Lick, had been donated to the American Philosophical Society in Philadelphia. Peale described the skull, noting that the "right horn is broken off, and all the fore part of the head; but from the fragment remaining, it is a reasonable conjecture, that the *Buffalo* to which it belonged was about 10 or 11 feet high." The core of the surviving horn "at the base measures 21 inches in circumference, and tapers very gently towards the extremity where it is broken off; so that the horn itself could not have been less than six feet in length."[10]

Peale asserted that the four extinct species had "been destroyed by some sudden and powerful cause; and nothing appears more probable than one of those deluges, or sudden irruptions of the sea, which have left their traces (such as shells, corals, &c.) in every part of the globe." By the early nineteenth century, it was widely believed that there had been a series of past oceanic deluges, of which Noah's Flood was the last. Peale concluded that although the exact cause of the animals' extinction was unknown, it had also brought about "the destruction of all those inhabitants from whom there might have been transmitted some satisfactory account of these stupendous beings, which at all times must have filled the human mind with surprise and wonder."[11]

While Rembrandt Peale and many other naturalists espoused extinction, Thomas Jefferson continued to hold that extinction was impossible, although a species might vanish from a portion of its original geographic range. Jefferson, for example, argued that the megalonyx was still alive, because the animal's total disappearance would have violated the inherent balance of nature:

In fine, the bones exist; therefore the animal has existed. The movements of nature are in a never ending circle. The animal species which has once been put into a train of motion, is still probably moving in that train. For if one link in nature's chain might be lost, another and another might be lost, till this whole system of things should evanish by piece-meal; a conclusion not warranted by the local disappearance of one or two species of animals, and opposed by the thousands and thousands of instances of the renovating power constantly exercised by nature for the reproduction of all her subjects, animal, vegetable, and mineral. If this animal then has once existed, it is probable on this general view of the movements of nature that he still exists.[12]

Jefferson suggested that although an animal species might have disappeared from the East, it could still be alive in the unexplored portions of the continent: "Our entire ignorance of the immense country to the West and North-West, and of its contents, does not authorize us to say what it does not contain."[13]

Once Jefferson became president, he was able to secure government funding for his long-envisioned exploration of the young nation's western lands. He engaged Meriwether Lewis and William Clark to lead an expedition beginning at the Mississippi River. In an 1803 letter to French naturalist Bernard Lacépède, Jefferson announced that the United States was "sending off a small party to explore the Missouri to its source, and whatever other river, heading nearest with that, runs into the Western ocean." Jefferson explained that one of the goals of the upcoming voyage of discovery would be to seek out knowledge of living "Mammoth, & of the Megatherium also."[14]

In the summer of 1803, Jefferson received a letter from Charles Willson Peale revealing that Cincinnati physician William Goforth had undertaken a fresh excavation for fossils at Big Bone Lick. Peale expressed his amazement over the reported size of some of Goforth's specimens: "I marval what are the teeth which he says weighs 19 or 20 pounds, can they be grinders. The largest I have seen belongs to Doctr. Wistar, its weight 10 pounds." Peale's description interested Jefferson, so he asked the westward-bound Meriwether Lewis (figure 20) to visit Goforth and examine his collection. Lewis dutifully stopped at Cincinnati on the way to meet William Clark at Louisville and prepare for their upcoming expedition.[15]

In October 1803, Lewis reported that Goforth had amassed a large number of bones, tusks, and molars of the mammoth, as

Figure 20. Meriwether Lewis visited Big
Bone Lick to collect fossils for Thomas
Jefferson. (Library of Congress, Prints
and Photographs Division)

well as several molars "of the Asiatic Elephant or an anamal very
much resembling it." Goforth had presented Lewis with both a
mammoth molar and an "elephant" molar and had given him
permission to take a large tusk and any other bones from the
portion of Goforth's collection that was still at the Lick. Lewis
wrote that he would visit the Lick the next day and then send
Jefferson the "large tusk together with the two grinders before
mentioned, and such other specimines as I may be enabled to
procure, and which, I may think worthy your acceptance."[16]

The fossils that Lewis sent from Big Bone Lick were freight-
ed downstream for transshipment to the East Coast, but they
never reached Jefferson. A boat accident at the Natchez landing

consigned them to the bottom of the Mississippi River. One report suggested that a few of the fossils had been recovered, as "it is said that some of them have been worked-up, and were very beautiful ivory."[17]

When Lewis and Clark returned to the East following their 1804–1806 expedition, Jefferson learned that they had failed to find any living specimens of the mammoth, megatherium, or megalonyx. The president also learned, perhaps from Lewis, that Goforth's collection from Big Bone Lick included the clawed foot of a large animal, a fact that Jefferson relayed to Caspar Wistar in Philadelphia. Wistar, on behalf of the American Philosophical Society, wrote to Goforth in December 1806 and asked him for "a description of the Bones of a large animal with claws, which you have procured in the western country— The accounts which have been circulated by travelers respecting the size of the foot have particularly attracted our attention." Wistar's letter also requested details about the complete skull of the mammoth, the upper portion of which remained missing from the animal's reconstructed skeletons: "Being possessed of all the bones of that animal, except those of the head, we will only ask you for information of that part of the mammoth—but an account of all the other unknown bones will be interesting to us." Wistar ended by soliciting Goforth's opinion on the possibility of procuring more bones from the Lick and his advice on how that might be accomplished. Wistar asked Goforth to address his answers directly "to the President of the U.S. who is President of the Society."[18]

As requested, Goforth replied to Jefferson in Washington, D.C., probably in early 1807 (the letter was undated). Goforth drew on his memory to answer Wistar's inquiries about the fossils, since the specimens were no longer in his possession. He described the bones of the claw-bearing foot, which "nearly filled a flour barrel." Goforth, however, could shed no light on the upper portion of the mammoth head, because his mammoth skull had consisted of only the upper and lower jaws. Goforth recalled that he and his party had collected as many loose mammoth molars "as a wagon and 4 horses could draw," and a number of "Elephant" molars "ribbed transversely on the masticating surface." A 100-pound tusk had measured twenty-one inches in circumference and ten and a half feet long. A femur "of a monstrous size" had been neither weighed nor measured. Vertebrae, when arranged in order and allowing for cartilage, had produced a column nearly sixty feet long, although Goforth was "not confident the bones all belonged to one animal." A twenty-one-pound horn had measured five feet long. Several bones of unidentified animals completed the list of specimens that he remembered from the collection.

Goforth recounted that he had gathered the fossils in 1803 while searching the Lick for a complete mammoth skeleton to sell in Europe. He wrote that although some of the large bones had been collected from the Lick's surface, most of the big specimens had been uncovered by digging "through several layers of small bones, in a stiff blue clay, such as deer; elk; buffalo and bear bone, in great numbers, many of them much broken, below which was a strata of gravel and salt water, in which we found the large bones, some nearly 11 feet deep in the ground." Goforth reported that before he could collect the remains of an entire mammoth skeleton, permission to dig had been withdrawn by the agent for David Ross, the Lick's owner.

Goforth concluded his letter by offering the American Philosophical Society his services in the recovery of bones for the society's collection: "I have long entertained a sanguine hope of bettering my circumstances by procuring skeletons, provided I could obtain permission to prosecute my search." He suggested that it "may be in the power of your learned body to produce me this permission, and if the society would wish collections of the bones of these nondescripts for their own use, I would undertake to superintend the collection and forward it to Philadelphia, or elsewhere, for such compensation as the Society should think proper." Goforth thought that a party of ten to twelve workers, provided with food and liquor, would be able to search the entire Lick. He estimated an expense of "about $1.25 each man per day; we could take provisions from this town, or take a hunter to kill for us."

As mentioned earlier, Goforth did not even know the whereabouts of his specimens when he wrote to Jefferson. Goforth's letter explained the reason for his ignorance about their current location: "The bones I collected were unfortunately intrusted to the care of a person who descended the Mississippi with them some months since; whether he proceeded to Europe with them, I am ignorant, as from accident or some other cause, I have received no account either of him or them."[19]

Some years later, the fate of Goforth's collection was revealed in *The Navigator*, an Ohio River guide published in Pittsburgh. An entry in the guide recounted the temporary storage of Goforth's Big Bone Lick specimens and their theft by Irishman Thomas Ashe (also known as Ash and Arvil), who subsequently claimed to be the collector and owner of the fossils:

In 1804 or 1805 he [Goforth] conveyed about 5 tons of these bones to Pittsburgh with a view of transporting them to Philadelphia and sell[ing] them to Mr. Peale, or to the American Philosophical Society. The bones, however, remained in Pittsburgh some time.

Mr. Ash had passed through Pittsburgh and descended to Cincinnati. There learning that Doctor Goforth had a very valuable collection of Big Bones he soon ingratiated himself into the Dr.'s graces, and entered into written articles with him to become his agent for the sale of the bones, by being allowed a specified part of the clear profits of sale, and New Orleans being fixed upon as the market for their disposal. Accordingly, Mr. Ash returned to Pittsburgh in 1806–1807 with an order from Dr. Goforth for the bones. They had been deposited with the late Dr. Richardson, who delivered them to Mr. Ash or Arvil, the name he then went by. The bones were boated to Cincinnati, under the command of Mr. Ash, thence he proceeded to New Orleans, where he made a feint to sell them, and was offered seven thousand dollars for them. He observed that the sum was not ⅒ of the value and from New Orleans shipped them to London, where, no doubt, he has accumulated an immense fortune by exhibiting that great natural treasure of curiosities to the court of that metropolis, while their real owner here is laboring under all difficulties of the loss of so valuable a property.[20]

Ashe, in fact, did not receive "an immense fortune." In 1806, he sold Goforth's Big Bone Lick fossils for 200 pounds to the Liverpool Museum. The museum's exhibit of the collection, which consisted of ten boxes of unassembled specimens, was accompanied by a booklet listing the fossils and containing Ashe's interpretive comments, many of which were plagiarized from George Turner's description of the mammoth. The first box held "the principal part of the head of a carnivorous animal." The skull displayed high-coned molars and the seating points of muscles that, "from their depth, must have given violent action to the nostrils and lips." The second box held vertebrae, and the third contained "ponderous and perfect" leg and pelvic bones. The clawed foot in the fourth box was highlighted as the most important structure in the display: "The animal to whom it appertained, with superior agility and ferocity to the tiger, with a body, too, of unequalled magnitude and strength, must have been the terror of the forest and of man." The fifth box contained ribs whose size and shape suggested "that the animal was endowed with the gift of contraction: his ribs closing together like the sticks of a fan, he could spring forward, or make a

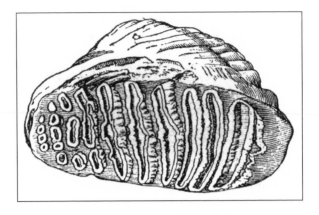

Figure 21. Elephant-like molar, one of the types of fossil teeth collected at Big Bone Lick by William Goforth. (Richard S. Lull, *Organic Evolution* [1917], 590)

mighty leap." Four unidentified bones from unknown animals were housed in the sixth box. The seventh and eighth boxes held dozens of teeth; one type was a molar "with high, double-coned processes, and interlocking fangs" that belonged to "the cruel carnivorous monster," and another molar (figure 21) had "parallel lines of enamel slightly indended," which denoted a "peaceable herbivorous animal." Ashe wrote that because the remains of the two species had been mixed together at Big Bone Lick and other sites, "they have hitherto been confounded together by writers, under the single appellation of mammoth bones." On the basis of the flat-surfaced molars of the second *incognitum*, Ashe reported that the animal had been a type of elephant—specifically, the extinct one known as the Siberian mammoth. A large tusk of the species, broken into three pieces, resided in the ninth box, and smaller tusks and horns of unidentified animals filled the tenth and final box.[21]

Ashe concluded the booklet by returning to the topic of the carnivorous mammoth. His description of the species was significantly different from that of Rembrandt Peale, who, three years earlier, had toured England with his skeleton of the mammoth before returning to the United States. Ashe believed that the animal had been terrestrial rather than semiaquatic, for he knew of no other carnivore that could account for the broken bones of elk, deer, and bison at Big Bone Lick. He depicted the mammoth as having clawed feet but lacking tusks, since tusks "would retard his progress through the woods, and gather too much wind when coursing his prey in the plains." Ashe estimated that the animal had stood twenty-five feet tall and measured sixty feet long—the same length calculated by Goforth, likely based on a reconstructed spine comprising vertebrae from more than one individual. Ashe characterized the beast's body as being "the best model of deadly strength, joined to the greatest agility." He ended his portrait of the species with a vivid description of the predator's feeding behavior: "from the force expressed by the visible seat of his muscles, his bounds must have been prodigious, enabling him to fall upon his prey, to seize it with his teeth; tear it with his claws, and devour it."[22]

After the exhibit closed, Liverpool Museum owner William Bullock gave away some of the specimens, used others for barter, and auctioned off the remainder. Several years later, he revealed that the clawed foot displayed at the museum was a fake that had been carved from the shoulder blade of an unknown animal. Coincidentally, Bullock later left England and moved to the United States, where he lived just twenty miles northeast of Big Bone Lick. Bullock's relocation was related to his Kentucky real estate investments, but he also took the opportunity to collect more specimens from the Lick.[23]

Chapter 9

━━━ ∾ ━━━

William Clark's Bountiful Collection

Go, wretch, resign the presidential chair,
Disclose thy secret measures, foul or fair,
Go, search with curious eyes for horned frogs,
'Mid the wild wastes of Louisianian bogs;
Or where the Ohio rolls his turbid stream,
Dig for huge bones, thy glory and thy theme.

—William Cullen Bryant, "The Embargo," 1809 (satirizing Jefferson's preoccupation with the Louisiana Purchase and Big Bone Lick)

At the beginning of the nineteenth century, French scientist Georges Cuvier highlighted Big Bone Lick as the primary source of remains of the American *incognitum:* "A huge quantity of its bones is found in an area on the banks of the Ohio River, in the west of the United States; almost all those in collections in Europe and America are from there." Cuvier also expressed his dissatisfaction with use of the term *mammoth* to denote both the Siberian mammoth and the American *incognitum:* "The second of these species is that to which the English and the inhabitants of the United States have transferred the name of *mammoth,* which properly belongs to the first. It is as large as the previous one, but its enormous teeth, armed with points, give it a distinctive character."[1]

In 1806, Cuvier assigned a new name to the American animal: *mastodon* (*mastodonte* in French). He constructed the title from the Greek terms for "breast" and "tooth," in reference to the conical protuberances on the grinding surfaces of the animal's molars. Cuvier thereafter restricted the title of mammoth to the fossil animal with the flatter grinding surfaces, similar to the molars of elephants.[2] It took a while for the new term to become universally known and accepted, and through the early decades of the nineteenth century, Americans continued to use *mammoth* when writing of the mastodon and *elephant* when referring to the elephant-like Siberian mammoth. American references to the elephant increased in the early 1800s as more of its fossils were collected at Big Bone Lick and other sites.[3]

Cuvier provided an authoritative account of the mammoth in the same paper in which he changed the animal's name to mastodon. He based his detailed description of the species on the animal's bones held in Paris, published figures of the Big Bone Lick specimens housed elsewhere in Europe, Charles Willson Peale's illustrations commissioned by Christian Michaelis, the description in Rembrandt Peale's pamphlet, and a drawing of the skeleton that the Peales had exhibited in England during 1802 and 1803. Cuvier used the accumulated data to conclude that the mastodon had not been a clawed predator of either terrestrial or aquatic prey. Instead, he determined that the mastodon had browsed on herbs, roots, and aquatic plants. In a summary statement of the animal's overall anatomy, Cuvier wrote, "the *great mastodon*, or *Ohio animal*, was very similar to the elephant in tusks and overall bone structure, except for its molars; it very probably had a trunk; it was no taller than an elephant, but somewhat larger, with slightly heavier members and a slimmer stomach."[4]

Cuvier's accompanying illustration of the mastodon's skeleton (figure 22) did not include the upper part of the animal's cranium, since that portion remained undiscovered. In a re-

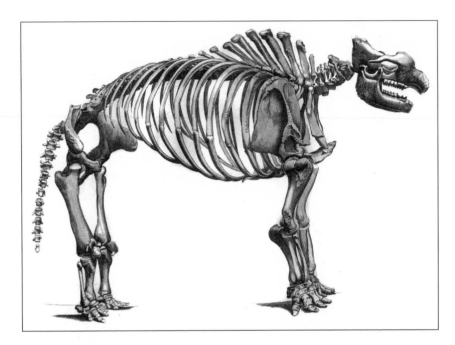

Figure 22. Cuvier's 1806 drawing of a mastodon skeleton minus the tusks and the as-yet undiscovered cranium. (Georges Cuvier, *Recherches sur les ossemens fossiles*, 3rd ed. [1825], vol. 1, p. 248, plate 5)

newed attempt to recover this missing part of the skull, as well as the animal's complete foot and any other fossil remains that were not represented in the American Philosophical Society's collection, President Jefferson organized an expedition to Big Bone Lick in 1807. Jefferson rejected William Goforth's offer to superintend the collecting party and instead engaged William Clark, co-leader of the recently completed Lewis and Clark expedition. Jefferson also secured permission to dig at Big Bone Lick from landowner and acquaintance David Ross.[5]

William Clark and his brother, George Rogers Clark, arrived at Big Bone Lick on September 6, 1807, to look for the requested specimens. A party of men was hired to assist in the dig, and tools were procured from Cincinnati. William Clark sent Jefferson a somewhat discouraging note from the Lick on September 20: "I have been employed two weeks at this place with *ten* hands searching for the bones of the Mammoth &c. without meeting with as much suckcess as I expected. This Lick has been pillaged so frequently that but fiew valuable bones are to [be] found entire." Nevertheless, Clark remained slightly optimistic about his chances of finding the desired fossils: "I feel much chagrined in not finding a great[e]r portion of the upper part of the head, and an entire paw of the Mammoth as Specimens to send forward to the Society, tho' I am not yet without hopes of finding those parts, and shall continue the Search one week longer."[6]

At the end of the three-week venture, Clark carried the collected specimens with him to Louisville and selected about 300 pieces to forward to Jefferson. The remainder of the collection was stored at his brother's home in Clarksville, across the Ohio River from Louisville. The specimens bound for Washington, D.C., via New Orleans, were shipped from Louisville on October 11. One month later, Clark used overland mail to send Jefferson an account of the several species collected by the expedition:

By letter of the 20th, of September from the Big Bone Lick, I done My self the honor of informing you the progress I had then made in the collection of certain bones at that place. After that time, Much to My chagrin No entire collection was made of the Paw, or the Great Pan of the head of the Mammoth. . . .

The different bones which I have Collected in this serch, are those of the Mammoth, the Eliphant, Two nondescript animals of the Sheep or Goat Species with horns bending down; the bones of one of those Animals much larger than those of their Class, the other small and May possibly be the female. An other animal with tapering horns connecting with the head at right angles, long and horizontal. I also found a Part of the head of an animal of the Buffalow or Cow Species, but no other bones which I can say with Certainty belongs to that Animal. . . .

Several bones of the horse were found at some depth under the surface in a stiff mud, a leg and foot bone of this animal which I have sent on to you was found in under mineing a high bank in the hard earth Eight feet Eight inches below the surface of the mud of the lick, and taken out in My Presents.[7]

Clark also wrote that Jefferson would soon receive all the fossils that were "curious and worthy of your inspection" and informed him that his brother held the surplus pieces, which could also be shipped if necessary.

The remainder of the letter was filled with Clark's interpretations of the collected specimens: "I will take the liberty of making a fiew desultory remarks and conjectures, the incorrectness of which I hope may be excused; they are intended more for enquiry than to place in oppersition My opinion with those better acquainted on those subjects." Contrary to the belief of Jefferson and many other Americans, Clark expressed the view that some animal species had become extinct: "Can any doubt exist after this of the existence in this Country at some former period of both the Mammoth and the Eliphant, as also of three or four other Animals Now extinct in the U. States! as well as the Horse and other Animals Common in America at this day." Clark believed that the vanished mammoths had been predators that fed on smaller salt-seeking animals that became stuck in the Lick's mud. He conjectured that as the mammoths "preyed upon those Mired animals, many of them must have Mired and perished in like Manner." Clark speculated that the large-bodied mammoth supplemented its meat diet by feeding on woody vegetation: "The Tongue which from every appearance was the great conductor of every species of food into the Mouth, may have been constructed as well to Collect the *twigs* and bough as to assist the Claws in seperating the flesh." Clark reported that the expedition had collected the molars of approximately forty mammoths, as well as the teeth of about six elephants. He described the elephant as an herbivore that visited the lick for salt "and like other animals mired and perished." Clark concluded his letter with a list of the specimens he had dispatched to Washington, D.C.[8]

Upon receiving Clark's letter, Jefferson rewrote and rearranged the inventory to produce a catalog of the fossil pieces arranged by species. Jefferson announced his plans to distribute the Big Bone Lick fossils in a December 19, 1807, letter to Caspar Wistar: "the great mass of the collection are mere duplicates of what you possess at Philadelphia, of which I would wish to make a donation to the National Institute of France which I believe has scarcely any specimens of the remains of these animals." Jefferson had been elected a foreign associate of the National Institute of France in 1801.[9]

On the same day that he wrote to Wistar, Jefferson sent Clark a letter thanking him for his services and informing him of the plan to distribute the numerous specimens from the Lick: "I see that after taking out for the Philosophical society everything that they shall desire there will remain such a collection of duplicates, as will be a grateful offering from me to the National institute of France for whom I am bound to do something." In order to make the gift as large as possible, Jefferson requested that the surplus specimens stored with George Rogers Clark be sent to him as well.[10]

Unfortunately, the additional fossils shipped from Clarksville to the White House were lost in transit, perhaps at Havana, Cuba. William Clark's original shipment from Louisville arrived safely in Washington on March 7, 1808, however. The delighted Jefferson had the Lick's fossils laid out in the White

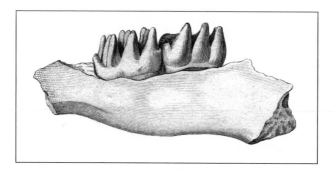

Figure 23. Fragment from a mastodon's lower jawbone collected at Big Bone Lick by William Clark. (Georges Cuvier, *Recherches sur les ossemens fossiles*, 3rd ed. [1825], vol. 1, p. 248, plate 3)

House storage area that later became the elegant East Room. Jefferson then invited Wistar down from Philadelphia, and together they divided the collection into three parts.[11] The largest group of fossils was sent to the American Philosophical Society in Philadelphia for further study by Wistar. A few of the mammoth and elephant specimens were added to the small natural history collection owned by Jefferson, who had personally paid all the expenses related to the collection and transportation of the fossils. The remaining pieces from Big Bone Lick were shipped to Paris for the National Institute of France (figure 23).

The National Institute deposited the Lick's fossils in the Muséum National d'Histoire Naturelle, also located in Paris. Some of the specimens in the collection provided Cuvier and his museum colleagues with evidence that the "elephant" of the New World was likely the same animal as the Siberian mammoth of the Old World. Following Cuvier's new terminology, the French scientists relabeled the *mammoth* specimens included in the 1808 gift as fossils of the *mastodon*. Jefferson may have become aware of the new name only when he received a thank-you note from the National Institute.[12]

Jefferson's second term as president ended in March 1809. In a May letter to Charles Willson Peale, Jefferson wrote, "I am totally occupied without doors, & enjoying a species of happiness I never before knew, that of doing whatever hits the humor of the moment without responsibility or injury to any one." In the same letter, Jefferson supported the renaming of the mammoth, stating that the title of mastodon "perhaps may be as good as any other, & worthy of adoption, as it is more important that all should agree in giving the same name to the same thing, than that it should be the very best which might be given."[13]

In a September letter to William Clark, Jefferson explained that the mammoth's new name had been derived from the breastlike protuberances on the grinding surfaces of the animal's molars. Jefferson also wrote that he had reexamined the teeth and now accepted that the species had eaten a plant-based diet. He stated that the shape of the molars "and the immense mass of their jaws, satisfy me this animal must have been arboriverous. Nature seems not to have provided other food sufficient for him, and the limb of a tree would be no more to him than a bough of a cotton tree to a horse."[14]

Eventually, Jefferson even reconsidered his position that animals authored by the perfect creator could not vanish from the earth. In an 1823 letter to John Adams, Jefferson wrote that divinely created earthly species and heavenly bodies could become extinct, to be replaced by new and different forms:

It is impossible, I say, for the human mind not to believe that there is, in all this, design, cause and effect, up to an ultimate cause, a fabricator of all things from matter and motion, their preserver and regulator while permitted to exist in their present forms, and their regenerator into new and other forms. We see, too, evident proofs of the necessity of a superintending power to maintain the Universe in its course and order. Stars, well known, have disappeared, new ones have come into view, comets, in their incalculable courses, may run foul of suns and planets and require renovation under other laws; certain races of animals are become extinct; and, were there no restoring power, all existences might extinguish successively, one by one, until all should be reduced to a shapeless chaos.[15]

In 1815, Jefferson resigned as president of the American Philosophical Society, and Wistar was elected to succeed him. Three years later, the society published the first of Wistar's descriptions of the Big Bone Lick fossils collected by Clark. Wistar's initial paper on the specimens had been read to the society in 1809 and was to have been published in its *Transactions* soon thereafter. Unfortunately, as had happened to so many fossil shipments from Big Bone Lick, Wistar's 1809 manuscript went missing. The society advertised in a Philadelphia newspaper for the return of the lost document, but when that was unsuccessful, it asked Wistar to reconstruct the manuscript. He eventually rewrote one portion of his paper, and it was published in *Transactions* in 1818. Wistar died the same year, so his other contributions regarding the Big Bone Lick fossils never appeared in print.[16]

Wistar's 1818 article was appropriately titled "An Account of Two Heads Found in the Morass, Called the Big Bone Lick, and Presented to the Society, by Mr. Jefferson." The first head he described was the one identified by Clark as having "tapering horns connecting with the head at right angles"; the second head was the smaller of the two skulls with "horns bending down." The first head largely consisted of the cranial portion of the skull, which, Wistar observed, had some features that resembled an elk and others that were similar to a moose (figure 24). Overall, the size of the fossil cranium, with its antler bases (Clark's "tapering horns"), was larger than that of either the elk or the moose. Wistar did not name the antlered animal, but his

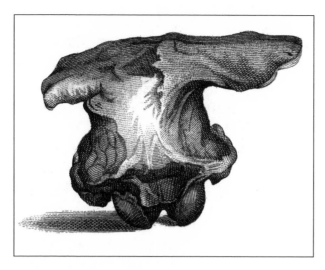

Figure 24. Skull of an elk-moose (posterior view) collected at Big Bone Lick by William Clark. (John D. Godman, *American Natural History* [1826], pt. 1, vol. 2, p. 197)

perception that the species exhibited a mingling of characteristics is corroborated by its present sobriquets: elk-moose or stag-moose. Even the animal's generic name, *Cervalces*, reflects that its features were intermediate between those of an elk (genus *Cervus*) and those of a moose (genus *Alces*). Its scientific name, *Cervalces scotti*, honors William Berryman Scott, who, in 1885, described a skeleton of the elk-moose that had been unearthed from a New Jersey bog.[17]

Since Clark's initial discovery at Big Bone Lick, fossils of elk-moose have been found in Canada and in the eastern half of the United States as far south as Arkansas and Oklahoma. These remains show that the males had complex, branching antlers that were broad and flat (females in the deer family lack antlers, except for reindeer and caribou). The animal had a face like that of an elk and a body that was slightly larger than that of a moose (figure 25). Because the moose-shaped animal likely fed in mires

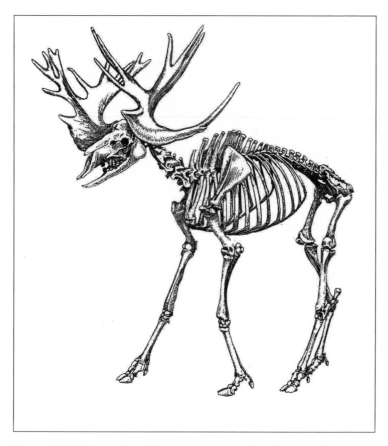

Figure 25. Skeleton of an elk-moose, a species first discovered at Big Bone Lick. (Oliver P. Hay, "The Pleistocene Period and Its Vertebrata," *Thirty-sixth Annual Report of Indiana Department of Geology and Natural Resources* [1911], 624, based on plate II in *Proceedings of the Academy of Natural Sciences of Philadelphia* [1885])

on moose-preferred vegetation, it may have visited Big Bone Lick for its wetland plants as well as for its salt. Elk-moose fossils date from 40,000 to 10,000 years ago.[18]

In his 1818 paper, Wistar described the second skull as having downward-curving horns, which made it "very different

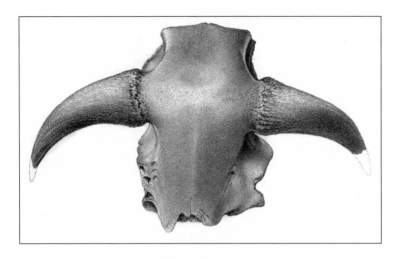

Figure 26. Skull of a helmeted musk ox (frontal view) collected at Big Bone Lick by William Clark. (Joseph Leidy, "Memoir on the Extinct Species of American Ox," *Smithsonian Contributions to Knowledge* [1852], vol. 5, art. 3, plate 4)

from that of any animal now known here" (figure 26). In terms of present-day animals, he decided that the head was most like that of an American bison in certain aspects: the general shape of the skull, the conical shape of the horns, and the lateral attachment of the horns to the skull. Wistar concluded his account by suggesting that the unknown species was a member of the genus *Bos*, the taxonomic group that then included bison (bison were later placed in their own genus, *Bison*).[19]

In 1825, Dr. Richard Harlan, the first American zoologist to specialize in the study of vertebrate fossils, assigned the scientific name *Bos bombifrons* to Wistar's vanished bison species. However, over the next quarter century, other zoologists observed that the specimen from Big Bone Lick (along with similar skulls collected later from other fossil sites) more closely resembled the head of the tundra musk ox than that of the American bison. For one thing, musk ox horns curve downward,

Figure 27. Sculpture of a female helmeted musk ox and calf, a species first discovered at Big Bone Lick. (Cincinnati Museum Center)

whereas bison horns curve upward. In 1852, the preeminent American paleontologist Dr. Joseph Leidy reassigned the species to the genus *Bootherium*, a name he coined for the extinct musk ox, which displayed skull features different from those of the extant tundra musk ox.[20]

Today, *Bootherium bombifrons* is referred to by one of three common names: Harlan's musk ox, woodland musk ox, or helmeted musk ox. The last designation refers to the fusion of the horns along the midline of the male's skull to form a "helmet," in contrast to the narrow separation between the horns of the tundra musk ox. The body of the helmeted musk ox (figure 27) was taller and more slender than that of the tundra musk ox. Remains of the helmeted musk ox have been found in Alaska and western Canada and in the contiguous United States from California to New Jersey and south to Louisiana. The animal

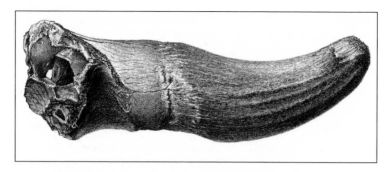

Figure 28. Horn core of an ancient bison (posterior view) collected at Big Bone Lick by William Clark. (Joseph Leidy, "Memoir on the Extinct Species of American Ox," *Smithsonian Contributions to Knowledge* [1852], vol. 5, art. 3, plate 2)

probably lived in Pleistocene boreal forests and grasslands, which were warmer than the habitat of the tundra musk ox, but it likely ate the same type of woody plants and meadow vegetation as the extant species. Helmeted musk ox fossils date from about 500,000 to 10,000 years ago.[21]

In addition to the two skulls described by Wistar, Clark's 1807 collection from Big Bone Lick included a small portion of a cranium with an attached horn core (figure 28). Clark identified the fossil as being from "the head of a Buffalo or Cow species." The specimen may have been described in Wistar's missing 1809 manuscript, but there was no reference to it in his 1818 publication. The fossil lay unnoticed in a Philadelphia museum cabinet until 1852, when Leidy identified it as a skull fragment from a previously unknown species that he named *Bison antiquus*, the ancient or antique bison.[22] Fossils of the ancient bison have since been found from California east to Virginia and from Alberta and Manitoba south to Texas and Louisiana. The remains date from 70,000 to 10,000 years ago. Specimens of the early ancient bison show horn spans greater than those of modern American bison, as well as larger bodies. Fossils of ancient bison from the last millennia of the Pleistocene display a trend toward the shorter horns and smaller bodies of modern bison. Because there is no clear delimitation in the size continuum from the ancient bison (*Bison antiquus*) to the modern American bison (*Bison bison*), the ancient bison is no longer recognized as a separate species; rather, it is considered an extinct subspecies of the American bison: *Bison bison antiquus*.[23]

Finally, Clark's collection from Big Bone Lick included the limb bones of a horse, another animal that was not mentioned in Wistar's 1818 article. Clark identified the bones as those of the present-day horse, although the deeply buried bones more likely belonged to a vanished species. Excavations by subsequent nineteenth-century collectors at the Lick yielded additional equine remains, including molars that proved to be from the extinct complex-toothed horse. This species, *Equus complicatus*, is distinguished from other extinct horses by the pattern of complex folding on the molar's grinding surface.[24] The first described fossils of the complex-toothed horse were collected from Gulf coast states, but later discoveries showed that the Pleistocene species lived in the east-central United States as well as in the South. The complex-toothed horse disappeared around 10,000 years ago, and the last of the other native horse species died out approximately 8,000 years ago. North America was thereafter void of any equine until the Spanish conquistadors imported the present-day horse, *Equus caballus*, to the New World.[25]

Following Clark's ample collection of specimens in 1807, institutions and individuals continued to gather fossils from the seemingly inexhaustible Big Bone Lick. None of the subsequent collecting parties found as many new species as did the 1807 expedition, however, reflecting both the completeness of Clark's work at the site and the fact that Pleistocene fossils were increasingly being found at other locations before they turned up at the Lick. Nevertheless, during the next two centuries, collectors at Big Bone Lick continued to unearth the remains of previously undetected species, including a ground sloth that was new to science.

Chapter 10

─── ❧ ───

The Faunal List Evolves

The quantity of fossil bones which appear to have been brought together at this place, and deposited within a very small area, is truly wonderful.
—William Cooper, 1831

In February 1818, Estwick Evans left his New Hampshire home and set off on a half-year, 4,000-mile western tour. Evans kept a travel log in which he recorded his observations of the places he visited, one of which was Big Bone Lick. Writing of the site's fossils, he repeated a popular explanation for the abundance of animal remains there: "Probably many of them fell into these licks, either by accident, by contention, or by their eagerness to get to the salt, and were thus destroyed." Evans also suggested other factors that may have caused the animals' demise: "Some too probably killed themselves by the quantity of salt water which they drank; and where such vast numbers were constantly assembling, many must have died in consequence of disease and old age."[1]

The accumulation of animal remains at Big Bone Lick continued to attract collectors during the second decade of the nineteenth century. John Clifford of Lexington unearthed bones from the Lick in 1816 or 1817, and Cincinnati's Western

Museum Society acquired specimens from the location in 1819. Two years later, however, Professor Constantine Rafinesque of Transylvania University discovered that the owner of the Lick and the adjacent health resort had prohibited fossil collecting at the site: "I found the actual owner a very surly man, who would no longer allow any excavations, having imbibed the notion that digging would take away the water from the spring, around which a pavilion and seats had lately been erected."[2]

The digging ban apparently did not remain in effect for very long, as there are many records of fossils being taken from the Lick during the 1820s. British visitor William Newnham Blane collected several fragments of a tusk from the Lick in 1822, referring to the site as "the Grave of the Mammoth." American explorer Stephen Harriman Long presented Philadelphia zoologist Richard Harlan with a selection of materials from Big Bone Lick that had likely been gathered in 1824. In 1825, Harlan described a new species of extinct tapir, *Tapirus mastodontoides*, on the basis of a tooth in the collection. A tapir is a semi-aquatic, donkey-size mammal that looks like a cross between a small elephant and a large pig.[3]

The identity of Harlan's fossil tooth was questioned by zoologist William Cooper, a wealthy New Yorker who spent his life in the unpaid pursuit of natural history materials. Cooper collected about seventy mastodon fossils from Big Bone Lick in 1828, including detached molars as well as one molar situated in a jaw fragment from a small mastodon, "probably the youngest yet discovered." Among the molars was one that matched the tooth in the juvenile mastodon's jaw and was "similar to the tooth, also from Big-bone Lick, described by Dr. Harlan, as having belonged to an extinct species of tapir." Cooper concluded that Harlan's identification of the tapir's tooth had been erroneous. After Harlan's death, his collection was transferred to the Academy of Natural Sciences in Philadelphia, where the renowned paleontologist Joseph Leidy examined the suspicious tooth. In 1859, Leidy agreed that it was "undoubtedly a first temporary molar of the Mastodon."[4]

Thus, Leidy authoritatively removed one tapir from the roll of extinct animals found at Big Bone Lick, but he erroneously added another, *Tapirus haysii*, to the list. In 1852, Leidy had coined that animal's scientific name and described it as a new species on the basis of a tooth found in North Carolina. In 1859, however, he garbled the data and mistakenly reported that the *Tapirus haysii* tooth had been obtained from Big Bone Lick. Leidy's error was carried forward, causing *Tapirus haysii* to appear on many rosters of the Lick's fossil fauna. In reality, there is no published verification of any tapir fossil occurring at the site.[5]

In 1828, while Cooper was collecting specimens at Big Bone Lick, Cincinnati physician Daniel Drake proudly wrote of the location's widespread reputation: "This spot has acquired a notoriety that is not even limited to the United States. Its name explains the nature of this distinction. No place in America, perhaps none in the world, has afforded an equal number of large fossil bones." In a footnote, Drake added, "New explorations would, no doubt, show that many bones yet remain, as Mr. Letton has, within the last two years, added a number, to the Cincinnati Museum."[6]

Frances Trollope, an English author who was temporarily residing in Cincinnati, provided a good description of Big Bone Lick's appearance and promise in 1828:

It appeared from the account of our travelers, that the spot which gives the region its elegant name is a deep bed of blue clay, tenacious and unsound, so much so as to render it both difficult and dangerous to traverse. The digging it has been found so laborious that no one has yet hazarded the expense of a complete search into its depths for the gigantic relics so certainly hidden there. The clay has never been moved without finding some of them; and I think it can hardly be doubted that money and perseverance would procure a more perfect specimen of an entire mammoth than we have yet seen.[7]

Cooper's 1828 excavations at the Lick did recover several bones from the mastodon (or "mammoth," as British writers still referred to the animal), but nowhere near enough to reconstruct a complete skeleton. Cooper's collecting also yielded molars of the true mammoth, two skulls of the helmeted musk ox, and a metacarpal bone of the Jefferson's ground sloth. The last discovery was not unexpected, since Cooper had seen the humerus of a Jefferson's ground sloth taken from Big Bone Lick at the Western Museum in Cincinnati. The species designation of both the metacarpal and the humerus would be called into question a century later by the Carnegie Institution's paleontologist Oliver Hay, but he also revealed that Princeton University owned a phalanx of the Jefferson's ground sloth that had been collected at the Lick.[8]

As related in chapter 8, Jefferson's ground sloth was first described by Thomas Jefferson in 1797. He named the animal *megalonyx* (Greek for "great claw"), because of its impressive, long claws. The cow-size ground sloth measured approximately nine feet long, including its stout tail. The woodland animal ate by rearing upright on its hind feet and tail to browse on twigs and leaves, using its forefeet to direct the foliage to its mouth (figure 29). Fossils of *Megalonyx jeffersonii* have been found in central Mexico, in western Canada, and throughout the conterminous United States, except for the desert and Rocky Mountain regions. Jefferson's ground sloth lived from around 150,000 to 10,000 years ago.[9]

Cooper's written account of his 1828 excavations at Big Bone Lick included a list of species represented in other recent collections from the site, such as the bear (species uncertain), horse

Figure 29. Sculpture of a Jefferson's ground sloth. (Cincinnati Museum Center)

(probably the complex-toothed horse), American bison, elk-moose, white-tailed deer, elk, caribou, and moose. Of the four extant members of the deer family, only the white-tailed deer and elk continued to reside in Kentucky after the end of the Pleistocene epoch 10,000 years ago; since that time, the boreal habitats of the caribou and moose have not existed in the state.[10]

From the 1820s through 1830, another major collection of fossils from Big Bone Lick was accumulated by Benjamin Finnell, owner of the Lick and its health resort. Finnell's collection of more than 300 bones, tusks, and teeth was exhibited in New York City in 1831. Benjamin Silliman, professor of geology at Yale College and editor of the *American Journal of Science and Arts*, wrote of his appreciation of Finnell's treasure: "I cannot refrain from attempting to convey to others something of the impression made upon my own mind on entering the room containing this astonishing assemblage of bones, many of which are of gigantic size." The fossils convinced Silliman "that races of animals formerly existed on this continent, not only of vast magnitude, but which must also have been very numerous; and the Mastodon, at least, ranged in herds, over probably the entire American continents."[11]

Among Finnell's discoveries was a unique pile of mastodon remains uncovered at the bottom of a hole that he excavated in 1830. According to an account of the find, mastodon bones "were laid around the outside of the wall and so inwardly to the center, and the skull placed on the top in the center." Every one of the bones was fractured, supposedly by the ancient Indians who had built the fossil pyramid. In Cooper's 1831 article on Big Bone Lick, he was skeptical of the presumed involvement by "aborigines, who, it was supposed, may have amused themselves by piling them up in this manner." Cooper suggested that the alleged symmetry of the bone heap might have been due to "the effects of the imagination in those who thought they saw such appearances of order."[12]

Mastodon remains from the bone pile and elsewhere in the Lick constituted more than half the fossils in the 1831 exhibit of Finnell's collection, according to a report by a committee of the New York Lyceum of Natural History. In addition, there were large numbers of teeth and bones from the Siberian mammoth and the horse. The latter species was likely the complex-toothed horse, since the committee noted that the equine specimens had been "found under circumstances that favour the belief of their being of equal antiquity with the extinct animals whose remains are associated with them in the collection." The other fossils in Finnell's collection were those of the American bison, helmeted musk ox, elk-moose, and Jefferson's ground sloth.[13]

The Lyceum committee reported that Jefferson's ground sloth (*Megalonyx jeffersonii*) was represented by at least two fossils in the Finnell exhibit—a detached tooth and a lower jaw

Figure 30. Sculpture of a Harlan's ground sloth, a species first discovered at Big Bone Lick. (Big Bone Lick State Park)

fragment holding four teeth. However, Richard Harlan identified the latter fossil as part of a jawbone of another species, *Megalonyx laqueatus*, and in 1840, British zoologist Richard Owen established that the jaw fragment was from a ground sloth of the genus *Mylodon*. Owen had identified the *Mylodon* genus from fossils collected by British naturalist Charles Darwin in South America, and he determined that the jaw fragment from Big Bone Lick represented a new species, which he named in honor of Harlan—*Mylodon harlani*.[14]

The current scientific name for Harlan's ground sloth (figure 30) is either *Paramylodon harlani* or *Glossotherium harlani*, depending on which taxonomist one considers to be authoritative. The ground sloth was more than eleven feet long and probably stood at least eleven feet tall when it reared up on its hind legs and massive tail. The stocky animal had pebble-like ossicles embedded in the skin of its neck, shoulders, and back, likely serving as protective armor against predators. It lived in open country, where it fed on grass, shrubs, and possibly roots that it unearthed with its large claws. Remains of the species have been found throughout the contiguous United States and central Mexico. Harlan's ground sloth lived from about 1.5 million to 10,000 years ago.[15]

Cooper reported in 1831 that the ground sloth's jaw fragment recovered by Finnell was in a very mutilated condition. Furthermore, the great majority of Big Bone Lick fossils showed "some mark of having been subjected to violent action." According to Cooper, "It is rare to meet with a single bone of the large animals, or of those smaller ones, that accompany them, that is not more or less bruised or broken." Cooper also cited the observations of William Bullock, the former owner of England's Liverpool Museum who had immigrated to Kentucky: "Many of the bones are much waterworn and broken; scarcely any that are not so, more or less. Some large fragments of the tusks of the elephant are worn quite flat and smooth, as if they had lain half buried in a water course, and worn down by the action from above."[16]

Cooper believed that the same water current that had damaged the Big Bone Lick fossils had also relocated them. He noted, for example, that a large number of loose teeth had been found piled together in a small area, proving "that the owners did not perish where these lie. In that case, the teeth would have remained in the respective heads, and have, consequently, occupied a much larger space." Cooper surmised that the water current was also responsible for the pile of mastodon remains uncovered by Finnell. Cooper adopted this view on the basis of an eyewitness account by Bullock, who had subsequently retrieved many additional specimens from the area bordering Finnell's fossil heap. According to Bullock, the bones "altogether formed a heterogeneous mass, lying horizontally, mixed with

angular and waterworn pieces of limestone of various sizes."
Among the intermingled bones, Bullock also found "fragments
of cane, small, unknown to me, and also fragments of broken
fresh-water shells, much resembling those now living in the
neighbourhood." The bone mass rested on a bed of blue clay in
which no animal remains were seen.[17]

Cooper concluded that the water had not carried the fossils
very far from their point of origin, or they would have exhibited
much more damage. Rather, he thought that the ancient animals had been living at or near the Lick "when the catastrophe
occurred, which seems to have extinguished their race." Cooper
apparently believed that this catastrophe had been a deluge of
biblical proportions that drowned the species and relocated
their remains at the Lick: "They appear to have perished by the
agency of water, which, after transporting their remains a mod-
erate distance, deposited them in a mass where they have since
been found. They were succeeded, after an interval, by the species which now inhabit the country."[18]

Finally, Cooper's comprehensive article included a local map
(see figure 4 in chapter 2) and the first detailed geologic description of the Big Bone Lick area, an important account that is
quoted here in full:

> The substratum of the neighbouring country, is a lime-
> stone, abounding in organic remains. This appears at the
> surface on the sides and tops of the hills, and along the
> banks of the great rivers. From it must have been derived
> the fragments mentioned in Mr. Bullock's account, as
> found accompanying the great bones. But at this lick, the
> valley is filled up to the depth of not less, generally, than
> thirty feet, with unconsolidated beds of earth of various
> kinds. The uppermost of these consists of a light yellow
> clay, which, apparently, is no more than the soil brought
> down from the higher grounds, by rains and land floods.

In this yellow earth are found, along the water courses, at various depths, the bones of buffaloes and other modern animals, many broken, but often quite entire.

Beneath this alluvial bed, is another thinner layer of a different kind of soil, presenting much of the character of a sediment, from a marsh or river. It is more gravelly, darker colored, softer, and contains remains of reedy plants, smaller than the cane so abundant in some parts of Kentucky, and shells of fresh water mollusca. It appears to be, in short, what is meant by diluvium, as distinguished from the alluvium, which forms the bed above it. In this layer, resting upon, and sometimes partially imbedded in a stratum of blue clay of a very compact and tenacious kind, are deposited the bones of the extinct species. Originally near the surface, they have been gradually covered by the accumulation of alluvial matter above them.

The depth of this alluvium is, however, variable. In some places it is very thin, and in others is liable to be entirely washed away by the inundations which are common here at some seasons of the year. When this takes place, the blue clay is left bare, and the bones exposed on the surface. It is in such situations, and along the banks and bed of the streams, that they have been found nearly or quite uncovered.[19]

Most of the "nearly or quite uncovered" fossils at the Lick were gathered up by collectors before the mid-nineteenth century. Prince Alexander Maximilian was made aware of this fact in 1832 while traveling by steamboat to Louisville. In an account of his journey down the Ohio River, the German prince wrote that he would have stopped at the renowned Big Bone Lick, "but some of our passengers, who were well acquainted with the country, assured me that there was now nothing to be seen there, nor was anything more found." Indeed, when the

Reverend Sayres Gazley stopped at the Lick in 1830, he noted that almost all the exposed fossils had been collected, but he also suspected that many buried specimens remained to be discovered: "Only a small part of the earth which contains these fossils, has yet been dug over. For centuries to come, these enormous bones, which have been the wonder of naturalists, will still be found."[20]

Chapter 11

Other Mammoth Changes

In the bottom lands one can scarcely dig down 3 or 4 feet
without being rewarded by finding some osseous relic of a
family of animals now either extinct or entirely unknown
in this latitude. What a commentary this fact is on the
transitory nature of mundane beings.
—S. E. J., 1876

Charles Lyell, one of the founders of modern geology, sailed
from England in August 1841 for a tour of the eastern United
States and Canada. His account of that one-year journey, _Travels
in North America_, includes a great deal of information on his
visit to Cincinnati. After arriving in the city in May 1842, Lyell
(figure 31) arranged for two local naturalists to guide him to
that "place of great geological celebrity in the neighbouring
State of Kentucky, called Big Bone Lick, where the bones of
mastodons and many other extinct quadrupeds have been dug
up in extraordinary abundance." The three men ferried across
the Ohio, rode southwest through a "magnificent forest" to the
Lick, and spent the remainder of the day exploring the site. The
party bedded down at a nearby farm, awoke to a breakfast of
broiled gray squirrels, and returned to Cincinnati "by another
route through the splendid forest."[1]

At the Lick, owner Benjamin Finnell called Lyell's attention

Figure 31. English geologist Charles Lyell visited
Big Bone Lick in 1842. (Horace B. Woodward, *History of Geology* [1911], i)

to a three- to four-yard-wide bison trail that was partially over-
grown by grass but, "sixty years ago, was as bare, hard, and well
trodden as a high road." Lyell learned from Finnell that "within
the memory of persons now living, the wild bisons or buffaloes
crowded to these springs, but they have retreated for many
years, and are now as unknown to the inhabitants as the mastodon itself." The American bison had disappeared from Kentucky, Ohio, and Indiana by about 1800.[2]

Lyell found the ground adjacent to the Lick's salt springs to be "so soft, that a man may force a pole down into it many yards perpendicularly." He believed that the boggy earth surrounding each spring, along with the behavior of animal herds, explained the abundance of bison bones and other fossil remains at the Lick: "It is well known that, during great droughts in the Pampas of South America, the horses, cattle, and deer throng to the rivers in such numbers that the foremost of the crowd are pushed into the stream by the pressure of others behind, and are sometimes carried away by thousands and drowned. In their eagerness to drink the saline waters and lick the salt, the heavy mastodons and elephants seem in like manner to have pressed upon each other, and sunk in these soft quagmires of Kentucky."[3]

Lyell reported that most of the Lick's fossils of extinct species had been excavated from a layer of soft, black mud containing a mixture of organic matter, freshwater and terrestrial mollusk shells, clay, sand, and gravel. In parts of the site, the fossil-bearing mud was covered by up to twenty feet of yellow, sandy clay that Lyell identified as the silt of the Ohio, a river "known to rise so high as to flow up the valley of Big Bone Creek, and, so late as 1824, to enter the second story of a house built near the springs." Lyell suggested that much of the river silt that had become stranded at the Lick was subsequently carried away by the meandering Big Bone Creek. He conjectured that the creek had also carried animal fossils away from the immediate vicinity of the salt springs and transported them to other areas of the Lick. Lyell formulated his displacement hypothesis after noting the locations where teeth were being collected and observing "the rolled state of some of the accompanying bones."[4]

Following Lyell's return to England, he presented a paper at the Geological Society of London concerning the age of the mastodon remains at Big Bone Lick and other sites in the United States and Canada. In the paper, Lyell reviewed the many findings that had led to his conclusion that the mastodon fossils were younger than the glacial drift (boulders, gravel, sand, and so forth) deposited by the last continental ice sheet. Therefore, the mastodon and associated extinct species had "lived after the deposition of the northern drift, and consequently the coldness of climate, which probably coincided in date with the transportation of the drift, was not as some pretend the cause of their extinction." Lyell did not suggest an alternative cause for the disappearance of these animals, perhaps because he could not calculate how long ago they had vanished. He considered the fossil remains to be very recent geologically but was unable to determine the number of years that had elapsed since their deposition. According to Lyell, the fossils "have been found at the depth of several feet from the surface, but we have no data for estimating the rate at which the boggy ground has increased in height, nor do we know how often during floods its upper portion has been swept away."[5]

Observations by Lyell, Georges Cuvier, and other early-nineteenth-century scientists established that certain animals had vanished when natural events and processes had changed their environments. The extinct species had then been replaced by new species in the altered environments. Although neither Lyell nor Cuvier could adequately explain how these new species originated, some of their colleagues tackled the vexing subject.[6]

Jean-Baptiste Lamarck worked alongside Cuvier at the Muséum National d'Histoire Naturelle in Paris. (Lamarck was one of the museum zoologists who, in 1796, had requested Big Bone Lick fossils from Charles Willson Peale.) Lamarck is best known for his 1809 book *Zoological Philosophy*, in which he postulated that new species arose from previous species due to the inheritance of acquired characteristics. Simply stated, alterations in the environment lead to alterations in an organism's habits; these, in turn, cause changes in its body. The bodily changes are then transmitted to succeeding generations, thus creating a new species. The chief objection to Lamarck's hypothesis is that a physical alteration produced during the life of a parent is not passed on to its progeny—for example, larger muscles developed by a parent are not inherited by its offspring. Owing to this and other problems, Lamarck's idea was largely displaced during the second half of the nineteenth century by a theory of evolution developed by British naturalists Charles Darwin and Alfred Russel Wallace.[7]

Darwin, who had been a student of both religion and natural history at Cambridge University, set off in 1831 on a five-year circumnavigation of the Southern Hemisphere. During the voyage, he observed the vestigial wings of flightless birds, the close similarities of island species to those on the nearest continent, and the sequences of fossils in South American deposits. Though a believer in the "creation of species" when he left England, Darwin had become a convert to the "evolution of species" by the time of his return in 1836. He married, settled outside of London, and spent the next several years doing research on the mechanism of species change. Finally, in 1859, at the urging of Lyell and other friends, Darwin presented his theory of natural selection in a book entitled *On the Origin of Species by Means of Natural Selection, or the Preservation of Favoured Races in the Struggle for Life*. At around the same time, Wallace also postulated that natural selection was the mechanism of evolution.

The Darwin-Wallace evolutionary theory consists of the following elements: Individuals within a species display variation. As these individuals struggle to live, those whose characteristics are best adapted to the environment survive and reproduce, while less-well-adapted individuals die without reproducing or produce fewer offspring. Over time, the unfavorable characteristics displayed by the less fit individuals disappear from the population, and the favorable characteristics become more common. In a changing environment, this process of natural selection results in a change in the population's characteristics and, finally, in the origin of a new species. Thus, an old species disappears from the fossil record either because it evolves into a new species or because it fails to change quickly enough to survive in the changing environment.[8]

The concept of evolution through natural selection initially met with much skepticism, if not downright hostility. However, within a decade of the publication of *Origin of Species*, most naturalists in the English-speaking nations had accepted the Darwin-Wallace theory. One of the first American proponents of organic evolution was paleontologist Nathaniel Southgate Shaler, a native of Newport, Kentucky, who served as director of the Kentucky Geological Survey from 1862 to 1879. Shaler pursued investigations at Big Bone Lick in 1868 and 1869, including a study of the American bison's evolutionary history. He shipped at least a ton of fossils from the Lick to the Museum of Comparative Zoology at Harvard University, where he was a professor of paleontology.[9]

Shaler's enumeration of the fossils unearthed by his crew included most of the animal species previously uncovered at the Lick. He also reported finding the remains of the giant bison, *Bison latifrons*, a species initially discovered a few miles from the Lick. However, Joel Allen, the nineteenth-century authority on living and vanished bison, was unable to distinguish any *Bison latifrons* fossils among the hundreds of pieces Shaler sent to the Harvard museum. Thus, the giant bison should be omitted from the Lick's faunal list until a verified specimen is found.[10]

Shaler wrote two major papers concerning his 1868–1869 investigations at Big Bone Lick. In one paper, he began with an overview of the Lick: "There the saline waters come up at various points over an area of about sixty acres, as rather large springs, each of which, unless artificially confined, oozes out through a large boggy area which may be fifty feet across." Shaler believed that the springs changed position through the ages, since much of the hard ground showed "evidence of having been at one time in the soft state which is now peculiar to the points immediately about the springs."[11]

In the other paper, Shaler reported, "When excavations are made near the existing outlets of the springs, we find remains of the large mammals brought into the country by man—the horse, cow, pig, and sheep." Likewise, remains of modern American bison were found near the surface at the current positions of the springs. The bison specimens were "very abundant, and not much more ancient in their appearance than the remains of the domesticated animals." Shaler concluded that modern American bison were recent immigrants to the region of the Lick and that "their coming was like an irruption in its suddenness."[12]

Shaler determined that the Lick's mastodon and mammoth fossils were buried primarily in older sediments. He theorized that early collectors had found some mastodon and mammoth remains at the surface of the Lick because the fossils had been exposed by the wallowing and trampling actions of the bison. He added that erosion produced by the meandering of Big Bone Creek likely played a role in uncovering the older fossils.[13]

Shaler discovered one place at the Lick that appeared to be free of past bison or stream disturbance. In an excavation at the location, the first fossils encountered were American bison bones at a shallow depth. Digging deeper, he unearthed the remains of other extirpated animals (e.g., caribou and moose) and, finally, those of extinct animals (e.g., helmeted musk ox, mastodon, and mammoth). Based on these findings, Shaler reasoned that the caribou and helmeted musk ox had vanished from the Lick before the modern American bison arrived at the site. He likewise concluded that the mastodon and mammoth predated the modern American bison and that the intermingling of the remains of all three animals at some locations was "clearly due to the degradation of the original deposits and the consequent displacement of the bones of the elephants."[14]

Shaler believed that the species preceding the modern

American bison had arrived at the Lick during the last glacial period and survived for an unspecified period after its closure: "It is probably in this belt of the country, just south of the southernmost line of glacial action, that the mass of creatures driven south by the ice-sheet remained, until that great invasion began to retreat to the northward." Shaler pointed to the present-day sub-Arctic range of the caribou to show that a warming climate had been responsible for the northward displacement of the Lick's cold-adapted mammals: "The disappearance from this region of this eminently boreal animal immediately after the passing away of the ancient elephants from the Mississippi valley, goes to confirm a conclusion to which we are led by many other facts, viz., that the climatic change that closed the period of the mammoths was from cold to warmth, and not, as is generally assumed, an alteration of the reverse character."[15]

Shaler taught his students at Harvard that changing climates and habitats had caused many species to vanish and be replaced by new species. He was aware that the concepts of both extinction and evolution contradicted the Judeo-Christian belief that all species had been perfectly created by God and would continue to exist unchanged until the end of the world. The professor enjoyed telling the story of a quiet old man who had regularly watched the crew excavate bones from the Lick. The observer remained silent until the day skeletal pieces of an extinct species were uncovered. As fragments of the animal were dug out, the man exclaimed, "That knocks Moses." He then left the Lick and never returned.[16]

During the decades following Shaler's investigations, fossils destined for museums continued to be taken from the Lick. In 1877, Dr. Christopher Graham of Louisville's Free Museum of Kentucky reported excavating wolf, cougar, and bear remains, as well as bones of species that had previously been found at the site. Graham believed that the predator species had come to the Lick to feed on the site's herbivores. Beginning in 1890, William Behringer gathered animal fossils from Big Bone Creek and Gum Branch; these were later donated to the William P. Behringer Memorial Museum (now the Behringer-Crawford Museum) in Covington, Kentucky. American historian Reuben Gold Thwaites, while visiting the Lick in 1894, viewed newly unearthed bones "on exhibition in the neighboring village, preparatory to being shipped to an Eastern museum."[17]

Cincinnati scientist John Uri Lloyd published a short report in 1904 concerning the length of time that an exposed fossil at the Lick had remained intact:

> Near the farm of my father-in-law, Mr. Thomas Rouse (born 87 years ago near Big Bone), on the side of a hill lay the shoulder blade of a mammoth. This blade had been upended, the base upon the ground, the blade against the trunk of an oak. So large was it that when Mr. Rouse was a boy, in the beginning of the last century, he stood under it to keep out of a summer shower. The bone fell upon the earth. It was attacked by wild beasts of various kinds that consume bone materials. It was disintegrated by the action of the air and frost and water. It crumbled, and before Mr. Rouse attained middle age had entirely disappeared.[18]

Although this was only a single bone, it suggested that an exposed fossil at the Lick would survive in the open for only a few decades. Rouse's story was consistent with Shaler's conclusion that the mastodon and mammoth remains found at the surface had not lain there since the Ice Age but had eroded out of the underlying sediments much more recently through the actions of water and bison herds.

A previously unrecorded mammoth species was added to the Lick's faunal list in 1923. Surprisingly, this was not the result of an examination of newly collected remains; rather, these fossils were found at the Academy of Natural Sciences in Philadelphia,

Figure 32. Woolly mammoth. (Richard S. Lull, *Organic Evolution* [1917], 602)

where they had probably been housed for more than a century. In a 1923 publication, paleontologist Oliver Hay revealed that the museum's Big Bone Lick collection contained molars from the Columbian mammoth as well as the woolly mammoth (the modern name for the Siberian mammoth). Prior to Hay's announcement, it had been presumed that the woolly mammoth (figure 32) was the sole source of the Lick's mammoth teeth.[19]

The Columbian mammoth had initially been recognized at other fossil sites in the mid-1800s based on the surface pattern of its molars, which is slightly less complex than that of the woolly mammoth. In the mid-1900s, fossils of the most recent Columbian mammoths began to be ascribed to another species—Jefferson's mammoth—owing to an increased number of ridges on the teeth. Some paleontologists now believe that the last animals of the Columbian mammoth lineage constitute the Jefferson's mammoth species, but others do not recognize Jefferson's mammoth as being distinct from the Columbian mammoth. Further complicating the identification of mammoth remains is the fact that the molars of all the mammoth species closely resemble one another. Therefore, a detailed study is required before any mammoth fossil from the Lick can be definitively ascribed to one of the three mammoth species: woolly, Columbian, or Jefferson's.[20]

The woolly mammoth, *Mammuthus primigenius*, inhabited the tundra and boreal forest of Eurasia beginning about 250,000 years ago. The species extended its range east into North America by 100,000 years ago, spreading through much of Canada and the United States; it became extinct about 11,000 years ago. The mammal measured up to ten feet tall at the shoulder, had upcurved tusks, and wore a coat of long hair over a thick undercoat. The body structure and coat of the woolly mammoth are well known from European Paleolithic cave art and from the thousands of frozen carcasses that have been dug out of the melting Arctic permafrost.

The Columbian mammoth, *Mammuthus columbi*, was a North American animal that stood up to thirteen feet tall at the shoulder and had gently curved tusks. The animal lived from about 1 million to 11,000 years ago (or earlier if the end of its lineage became a separate species, the Jefferson's mammoth). Fossils of the mammal have been found from Alaska to Nicaragua. Because the Columbian mammoth generally occupied warmer localities than the woolly mammoth did, it is presumed that the animal was covered with only a thin layer of hair that may have been supplemented with a winter undercoat. According to Greg McDonald, former vertebrate paleontologist at the Cincinnati Museum of Natural History (Cincinnati Museum Center), most scientists currently believe that the Columbian mammoth is the only mammoth species present in the Big Bone Lick fossil fauna.

Jefferson's mammoth, either a separate species (*Mammuthus*

jeffersonii) or a late form of the Columbian mammoth, appeared at some indeterminate time during the Ice Age and lived until approximately 11,000 years ago. Remains of the mammal have been found from Canada to Mexico. Jefferson's mammoth stood up to twelve feet high at the shoulder and had slightly incurved tusks.

The fossil molars of mammoths are similar to the teeth of elephants; thus, it is believed that mammoths grazed mainly on grasses and other nonwoody plants and ate the fruits, leaves, twigs, and bark of shrubs and trees. In contrast, the American mastodon, *Mammut americanum*, used the distinctive conical cusps on its molars primarily for browsing on the leaves and twigs of boreal trees, mostly conifers, and for feeding on nonwoody terrestrial and aquatic plants. The digestive tracts of American mastodons found preserved in sphagnum bogs have been filled exclusively with such plant matter, evidence that the mastodon was neither the carnivore nor the omnivore depicted by some early naturalists.

A coarse hair coat covering a layer of finer hair insulated the American mastodon, which lived in cold woodlands, grasslands, and wetlands. The mastodon (figure 33) stood up to ten feet high at the shoulder and bore tusks that curved gently upward. The rare specimens of the mastodon's complete skull show that it lacked the high-domed top of a mammoth's head, although the mastodon's skull was larger overall than that of the mammoth. Also, in contrast to the mammoth, the mastodon's skull was carried more horizontally, and its body was more heavily muscled. The American mastodon lived over a long span of time, from approximately 3.75 million to 11,000 years ago. Skeletal pieces of the animal have been found at sites throughout North America north of central Mexico, but probably the greatest number of mastodon fossils has been collected at Big Bone Lick.[21]

Willard Jillson of the Kentucky Geological Survey uncovered mastodon bones at the Lick in 1924, along with a mastodon

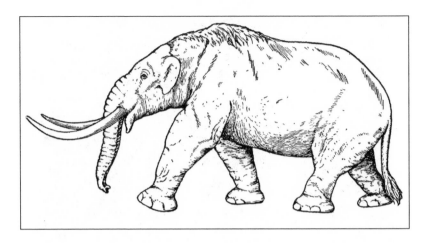

Figure 33. American mastodon. (Richard S. Lull, *Organic Evolution* [1917], 599)

or mammoth tusk fragment, a mammoth tooth, and bison remains. In 1928, University of Kentucky professors William Funkhouser and William Webb were the first to report that remains of the extinct flat-headed peccary had been collected at the site. Sixty years earlier, Shaler may have found fragments of the flat-headed peccary's humerus and lower jaw, but the pieces had tentatively been identified as those of the extant collared peccary and domestic hog, respectively. Because Funkhouser's 1925 book, *Wild Life in Kentucky*, did not include Big Bone Lick in its list of statewide locations of the flat-headed peccary, the remains were probably found sometime after that date.[22]

Peccaries of the New World are related to pigs of the Old World, but peccaries have larger heads, shorter necks, and upper canines (tusks) that point downward instead of curving upward. The flat-headed peccary (figure 34), *Platygonus compressus*, lived from about 1.8 million to 12,000 years ago. The browsing omnivore stood two and a half feet high at the shoulder and displayed features adapted for life in open areas, such as lateral placement of the eyes, long legs, and a dust-filtering nasal cavity.

Figure 34. Sculptures of flat-headed peccaries. (Cincinnati Museum Center)

Fossils of the species have been found from northern Canada to Mexico and from coast to coast.[23]

Flat-headed peccary specimens reportedly were included in the fossil collection that Parker Melvin amassed from the Lick during the 1940s and 1950s and donated to the Big Bone Lick State Park Museum. However, Greg McDonald could not locate any flat-headed peccary fossils in any collection from the Lick housed at the Big Bone Lick State Park Museum or elsewhere. Given the absence of confirmed specimens, the species should be deleted from the Lick's faunal list until peccary materials are found and verified.[24]

The mid-twentieth century saw continued collecting at Big Bone Lick. Ellis Crawford, director of Covington's William P. Behringer Memorial Museum, unearthed a mastodon jawbone from the channel of Big Bone Creek in 1960. Edwin Way Teale, a naturalist who visited the Lick in the winter of 1962, reviewed the record of collecting at the location and concluded with a statement that soon proved correct: "The fossil lode at Big Bone Lick is far from exhausted."[25]

Chapter 12

Agents of Extinction

[The] number of animals that met disaster and death at Big Bone Lick must be conceded to run far beyond the hundreds and into the thousands of individuals. Such a profusion of bones! Such a multiplicity of individuals! Such a charnel house in nature!
—Willard Rouse Jillson, 1936

A field party led by personnel from the University of Nebraska State Museum began a five-year study at Big Bone Lick in July 1962. The investigation was cosponsored by the State Museum, the U.S. Geological Survey, and the William P. Behringer Memorial Museum. Ellis Crawford of the Behringer Museum collected several prehistoric Native American artifacts, the oldest being an Early Archaic projectile point between 8,000 and 10,000 years old. The primary purpose of the study, however, was to outline the succession of mammalian fauna at the Lick since the Wisconsinan glacial period. The field party uncovered and identified about 2,000 vertebrate remains during the summer of 1962 and undoubtedly collected several thousand more specimens before the fieldwork ended in June 1967.[1]

Progress reports appeared periodically during the study, but an anticipated 1976 monograph on the results and conclusions of the project was never published. In 1981, while studying early

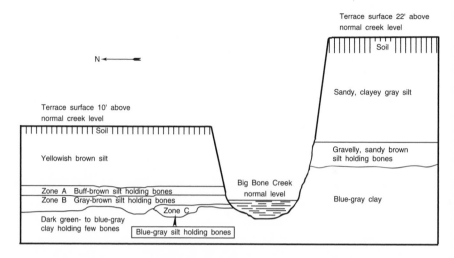

Figure 35. Diagrammatic cross section based on excavations at Big Bone Lick. (Adapted from C. Bertrand Schultz et al., "Paleontologic Investigations at Big Bone Lick State Park, Kentucky: A Preliminary Report," *Science* 142 [1963]: 1168)

Indian sites at the Lick, Kenneth Tankersley excavated profile sections in the same areas examined by the Nebraska scientists. Tankersley formulated and published his own explanations for how the sediment layers had developed and the fossil deposits had come about.[2]

One of the museum's 1962 excavations, designated KEN-2, was opened on a terrace along the south bank of Big Bone Creek's "New Cut," on the island that existed in 1830 prior to the filling of the stream's old channel (see figure 4 in chapter 2). The surface of the terrace was about twenty-two feet above the normal water level of the creek (figure 35). The upper twelve and a half feet of the terrace fill consisted of a soil complex and underlying sandy, clayey, mottled gray silt with rusty iron staining. From twelve and a half to sixteen and a half feet below the terrace surface, bones were found in a calcareous, gravelly, sandy, brown silt layer. The fossil remains were those of mastodon, mammoth, ancient bison, horse (probably complex-toothed horse), musk ox (probably helmeted musk ox), ground sloth (probably Harlan's ground sloth), elk-moose, deer, and bear. Below the bone-bearing layer was a compact, calcareous, blue-gray clay.[3]

Tankersley identified the underlying blue-gray clay as being from 18,000 to 19,000 years old, based on the estimated ages of similar sediments at other regional sites. The lake-deposited clay had accumulated in the Big Bone Creek valley due to the damming of the stream's mouth by Wisconsinan glacial outwash debris in the Ohio River channel. The clay deposition ended following the erosion of the glacial debris dam, after which the clay became covered by the brown silt layer containing coarser materials washed from the Big Bone Creek watershed. Among these materials were the bones of animals that had died while visiting the valley of the Lick. Finally, the bone-bearing, brown silt layer was buried under several feet of gray silt that had likely been deposited during Ohio River flooding events.[4]

Radiocarbon dating of wood associated with the bones at KEN-2 yielded an age of 10,600 ± 250 years. However, a helmeted musk ox skull that William Clark had taken from the Lick in 1807 was found to be many thousands of years older. In 1967, an age of 17,200 ± 600 years was determined for the plant-bearing silt found in the cranial cavity of that skull by U.S. Geological Survey scientist Frank Whitmore.[5]

KEN-1, another excavation opened by the University of Nebraska State Museum in 1962, was located on the floodplain of Big Bone Creek. The dig site was on a terrace along the north bank of Big Bone Creek's "New Cut," in the area where fossil excavation sites were shown on Cooper's 1830 map (see figure 4). The surface of the terrace was ten feet above the normal creek level (see figure 35), but it still flooded for a brief period during the summer of 1962. Digging downward from the surface, a seven-foot layer of soil and water-deposited, yellowish brown silt was removed before the first bones were encountered. The bones were found in a layer of buff-brown, mottled silt extending from seven to eight and a half feet below the surface, designated Faunal Zone A. Zone A contained bones of deer, modern American bison, and domesticated horse, cow, pig, and dog. The zone also held a few bones of extinct animals, probably discarded by earlier fossil collectors. Besides the animal remains, the collecting party found fragments of china and crockery, bricks, building stones, hand-hewn boards, logs, branches, and seeds. The unearthed cultural materials from the early 1800s showed that the seven feet of water-deposited silt above Zone A had accumulated over a period of about 150 years.[6]

Faunal Zone B, a layer of dark gray to dark brown, sandy, humic silt, was located from eight and a half to between ten and eleven feet below the surface. Radiocarbon dating of two pieces of wood collected from the zone indicated that the specimens were from the 1700s. Animal fossils discovered in Zone B included abundant remains of modern American bison, along with the bones of deer and elk. The zone also contained fragmentary bones of caribou, mastodon, mammoth, bison (probably ancient bison), horse (probably complex-toothed horse), and musk ox (probably helmeted musk ox). The bone fragments had apparently been subjected to stream action that transported them from other locations.[7]

Faunal Zone C, of variable thickness, was a layer of blue-gray, sandy silt situated from ten to eleven to at least fifteen feet below the surface. Zone C held bones of caribou, mastodon, ancient bison, complex-toothed horse, musk ox (probably helmeted musk ox), ground sloth (probably Harlan's ground sloth), and elk-moose. The zone may have held the remains of additional species; some of the fossils had yet to be identified by the time of the study's last published progress report.[8]

Beneath Zone C, occasional bones were found in a dark greenish to bluish gray clay that extended to at least twenty-nine feet below the surface. Due to its position and color, this clay at the bottom of KEN-1 was believed to be the same age as the clay found at the bottom of KEN-2. However, the gray silt found above the Pleistocene (Zone C) fossils at KEN-2 was absent from the same level at KEN-1, likely because it had been washed away by past lateral movements in the floodplain by Big Bone Creek and Gum Branch. The KEN-1 excavation's bone-bearing Zone C was, instead, buried under sediment layers that had been deposited after stream erosion removed the gray silt.[9]

In 1966, an excavation designated KEN-3 was started at a location just southeast of the "Big Lick" salt springs shown on Cooper's 1830 map (see figure 4). A pioneer-era saltworks and associated historic materials were unearthed at the site, including a barrel from the early 1800s. A progress report states that paleontologic and "important" geologic data were obtained at KEN-3, but such information has remained unpublished since the conclusion of the project in 1967.[10]

In 1981, Tankersley dug a pit adjacent to the KEN-3 excavation site and uncovered a pile of disarticulated bones from a modern American bison. Cut marks on some of the bones and the nearby presence of fleshing tools led him to believe that the animal had been killed and butchered at the site. He also deduced that the hunters had been a group of Fort Ancient Indians, based on two diagnostic pottery fragments found in the vicinity and a radiocarbon date determination of AD 1420 ± 105. On the basis of his discoveries and those of archaeologists in other eastern states, Tankersley calculated that the modern American bison had entered the Big Bone Lick region in approximately 1450 and had disappeared from the area in about 1800. A radiocarbon sample from a bison molar collected at the lick in 1993 yielded a date of AD 1830 ± 55.[11]

In 1962, when the Nebraska scientists identified domesticated dog remains at the KEN-1 site, the canine species became the last previously unrecorded mammal to be excavated from Big Bone Lick. The total number of mammals that paleontologists have found at the Lick presently stands at twenty species: seven extinct, six extirpated, two resident, and five domesticated (table 1). Two of the extirpated species, moose and caribou, moved north out of the region as the climate warmed at the end of the Pleistocene epoch. White-tailed deer, American black bear, American bison, gray wolf, elk, and cougar disappeared in the early nineteenth century due to overhunting. Only the deer and bear later returned to the Lick's vicinity after hunting laws were established.[12]

TABLE 1. MAMMAL SPECIES EXCAVATED AT BIG BONE LICK

Common Name	Scientific Name
Extinct species	
Helmeted musk ox	*Bootherium bombifrons*
Elk-moose	*Cervalces scotti*
Complex-toothed horse	*Equus complicatus*
American mastodon	*Mammut americanum*
Columbian mammoth	*Mammuthus columbi*
Jefferson's ground sloth	*Megalonyx jeffersonii*
Harlan's ground sloth	*Paramylodon harlani*
Extirpated species	
Moose	*Alces alces*
American bison	*Bison bison*
Gray wolf	*Canis lupus*
Elk	*Cervus elaphus*
Cougar	*Puma concolor*
Caribou	*Rangifer tarandus*
Resident species	
White-tailed deer	*Odocoileus virginianus*
American black bear	*Ursus americanus*
Domesticated species	
Cow	*Bos taurus*
Dog	*Canis familiaris*
Horse	*Equus caballus*
Sheep	*Ovis aries*
Pig	*Sus scrofa*

Climate change and human hunting—the factors responsible for the extirpation of extant species from the Lick—are believed to be major contributors to extinction as well. An additional cause of extinction may be interspecific competition that develops with the appearance of a foreign species. For example, the elk-moose may have vanished when it was displaced by a superior competitor—the moose that arrived in eastern North America during the Wisconsinan glaciation. Even if there is no competition between an invading and a native species, the invader might introduce a disease-causing microbe or parasite that sickens the resident population, leaving it susceptible to other environmental pressures, such as climate change and human hunting.[13]

There is ample evidence of climate change in North America since the Wisconsinan glacier, the last ice sheet to visit the Big Bone Lick region. Like all continental glaciers, the Wisconsinan formed during a period of global cooling when more snow fell in winter in the Arctic than melted in summer. The accumulating weight compressed the snow into glacial ice, which then spread southward across the continent. The Wisconsinan glacier came within thirty miles of the Lick, as evidenced by a moraine located a few miles north of the Ohio River in Hamilton County, Ohio. Radiocarbon dating of spruce logs buried in the county's glacial drift revealed that the advancing Wisconsinan ice sheet had knocked over the trees approximately 20,000 years ago. A few hundred years later, a warming climate caused the glacier to begin its retreat, as the ice at its margin melted away faster than the glacial ice pushed forward.[14]

Several studies have shown that boreal coniferous woodlands stretched many hundreds of miles south of the Wisconsinan glacial boundary. For example, paleoecologists have discovered evidence of boreal conifers in Kentucky and Tennessee sinkhole lakes. These lakes contain sedimentary records of pollen grains blown into the water from plants in the area. By analyzing the pollen composition at various radiocarbon-dated levels in the bottom sediments, the investigators determined that open woodlands of spruce and pine existed as far south as middle Tennessee until about 16,500 years ago.[15]

As mentioned earlier, the silt extracted from the helmeted musk ox skull collected by William Clark was found to be 17,200 ± 600 years old. It contained mostly spruce and pine pollen, the same pollen types prevalent in the Kentucky and Tennessee lake sediments from the same period. Today, boreal coniferous forests dominated by spruce and pine grow in regions that are cool and moist, so it is surmised that these climatic conditions existed for hundreds of miles south of the margin of the Wisconsinan ice sheet.[16]

Beginning approximately 16,500 years ago in middle Tennessee, the pollen percentages of spruce and pine diminished and those of deciduous trees increased, reflecting a postglacial warming trend. Deciduous trees were spreading north due to a lengthening growing season that allowed them to make enough food during the summer to last through winter, when they were leafless. The invading deciduous species eventually replaced the boreal conifers because their wide leaves were more efficient in capturing sunlight than the needle-shaped leaves of coniferous species. Pollen studies have determined that the coniferous-to-deciduous transition took place about 11,500 years ago in central Kentucky and approximately 10,000 years ago in the vicinity of Big Bone Lick.[17]

As the deciduous forest pushed northward, the boreal coniferous forest likewise advanced into higher latitudes, moving onto the land that was emerging from beneath the receding glacier. However, some of the plant species that had lived in the Late Pleistocene spruce-pine woodlands in the south-central states were probably unable to relocate successfully. Species react individually to limiting factors such as length of daylight, nutrient availability, and soil moisture. For this reason, not all the plant species that constitute a community are able to adapt to a new habitat at another site. Thus, the composition of the present-day boreal woodland community in Canada is believed to be different from that which grew in the south-central United States during the latter part of the Ice Age. If any of the missing plant species provided food for large mammals, starvation may have caused the extinction of some species in the boreal mammalian fauna. However, this famine hypothesis cannot be confirmed or refuted until more data are collected on the diets of the extinct herbivores and the climate-related relocations of the animals and their food plants. Gathering such information might be impossible.[18]

Perhaps some or all of the extinct species recorded at the Lick died off not due to the ecological effects of the warming postglacial climate but due to hunting by the Paleo-Indians. The Lick's seven vanished mammal species became extinct between 10,000 and 12,000 years ago, the approximate time that the Clovis people arrived south of the Wisconsinan ice sheet. These Paleo-Indians may have come from Asia by boating across the Pacific or by walking over the Bering land bridge from Siberia to Alaska. Alternatively, they may have migrated from Europe to North America by boating along or walking over the Late Pleistocene pack ice in the North Atlantic Ocean.[19]

Although other human groups probably preceded the Clovis people to the New World, these earlier cultures did not possess the large stone spear points used by Clovis hunters to bring down big game. Clovis spear points have been collected at Big Bone Lick, suggesting that the Paleo-Indians hunted animals there (figure 36). At other North American fossil locations, Clovis points have been found in direct association with animal remains, showing that the Paleo-Indians preyed on mastodons and mammoths as well as other large mammals. The lack of experience with intelligent, well-armed predators may have caused the rapid extermination of many species.[20]

Figure 36. Clovis projectile points collected at Big Bone Lick. (Stanley Hedeen, *Cincinnati Museum Center Scientific Contributions Number 1: Natural History of the Cincinnati Region* [2006], plate 24)

Like the famine hypothesis, the proposition that Paleo-Indian hunting led to the extinction of Late Pleistocene mammal species suffers from a lack of definitive evidence. More data are needed (but are probably unobtainable) concerning the population growth, population movement, food preferences, and hunting success of the Clovis people. However, it is an undeniable fact that the killing of animals leads to extinction. Studies in New Zealand and other Pacific islands have determined that many native species disappeared when their populations became the prey of prehistoric human groups.[21] And it is certain that hunting was responsible for the historic extinctions of the passenger pigeon and the Carolina parakeet, two eastern North American species that were once common at Big Bone Lick. The pigeon and parakeet were herbivorous birds that flocked to the Lick's brine. Both William Clark and Alexander Wilson, the father of ornithology in North America, made note of the

Figure 37. Carolina parakeet captured at Big Bone Lick, and three warbler species. (Alexander Wilson and Charles L. Bonaparte, *American Ornithology* [1876], vol. 1, plate 26)

great numbers of passenger pigeons and Carolina parakeets that frequented the salt springs. Wilson's portrait of a parakeet captured at the Lick was included in his epic work *American Ornithology* (figure 37). Wilson described the spectacle created by the parakeets during his 1810 visit to the site:

They came screaming through the woods in the morning, about an hour after sunrise, to drink the salt water, of which they, as well as the pigeons, are remarkably fond. When they alighted on the ground, it appeared at a distance as if covered with a carpet of the richest green, orange, and yellow; they afterwards settled, in one body, on a neighboring tree, which stood detached from any other, covering almost every twig of it, and the sun, shining strongly on their gay and glossy plumage, produced a very beautiful and splendid appearance.[22]

The nineteenth-century decline in both passenger pigeon and Carolina parakeet populations was due in part to the human destruction of their forest habitat, but it was mostly the result of intense hunting. The pigeon, once the continent's most abundant bird, was slaughtered for its tasty flesh. The parakeet was seldom shot for meat but was, instead, slain for its fashionable feathers, for sport, and for pest control. Known as the "winged rat," the parakeet was a hated agricultural pest that fed on fruit in orchards and grain in crop fields.[23]

The last verified wild passenger pigeon was shot in 1902 at an Indiana site a few miles north of the Lick, and the last known wild Carolina parakeet was taken in 1913 in Florida. The pigeon became extinct in 1914 when a caged female died at the Cincinnati Zoo, and the parakeet disappeared forever in 1918 when a captive male passed away at the same zoo. The pigeon and parakeet are among the approximately 200 birds and mammals that have vanished from the earth over the last four centuries, many of them driven to extinction by overhunting. Since 1600, the approximate extinction rates per century are 0.5 percent for birds and 1.0 percent for mammals, greatly exceeding the natural extinction rates reflected in the fossil record.[24]

In addition to the historic disappearances of the passenger pigeon and the Carolina parakeet at the hands of gun-bearing predators, several more species of deciduous forest animals could depart Big Bone Lick in the upcoming centuries due to human-induced climate change. Elevated temperatures brought about by increasing amounts of air pollution might cause some organisms to move to more northern latitudes. However, it is likely that some plant species would be intolerant of environmental factors in the new locations, so those plants and the animal species that depend on them would vanish. The same extinction scenario would play out in all the planet's ecological communities forced into higher latitudes by global warming. At the highest latitudes, global warming would cause the mass extinction of the world's present polar species.

The amount of atmospheric carbon dioxide, the major gas responsible for global warming, is increased by the combustion of fossil fuels. The burning of coal, oil, and natural gas in electricity-generating plants presently produces one-quarter of the human-caused carbon dioxide emissions. A promising method to remove this gas from the smokestacks of power plants is to capture and inject it into deeply buried geologic strata. One of the best North American geologic layers in which to sequester carbon dioxide is Mount Simon Sandstone.[25]

And so this book ends where it began. Mount Simon Sandstone may supply the brine for the salt springs at Big Bone Lick, the site that served as the birthplace of American paleontology and brought species extinction to the attention of the world. Now, the same geologic layer may play a role in averting increased extinction rates. Putting an end to global warming, as well as overhunting and other species-endangering human actions, will prevent living organisms from following the passenger pigeon and the Carolina parakeet into oblivion. Nothing can be gained by prematurely adding other species to the list of extinct animals that once gathered at Big Bone Lick.

Notes

Introduction

1. Humphrey Marshall, *The History of Kentucky* (Frankfort, Ky.: Henry Gore, 1812), 85–86.

1. Geologic Setting

1. Charles Lyell, *Travels in North America* (New York: Wiley and Putnam, 1845), 2:39–58; André Michaux, *Journal, 1793–1796*, in *Early Western Travels, 1748–1846*, ed. Reuben G. Thwaites (Glendale, Ky.: Clark, 1966), 3:36–37.

2. Paul E. Potter, *Exploring the Geology of the Cincinnati/Northern Kentucky Region* (Lexington: Kentucky Geological Survey, 1996), 21; Kenneth B. Tankersley, "Potential for Early-Man Sites at Big Bone Lick, Kentucky," *Tennessee Anthropologist* 10 (1985): 29.

3. R. A. Davis, "Big Bone! Kentucky's Original Stick-in-the-Mud," *Rocks and Minerals* 56 (1981): 116; Potter, *Exploring the Geology*, 20–26.

4. Potter, *Exploring the Geology*, 43–44.

5. Ibid., 12–14.

6. Sarah Johnson and William M. Andrews Jr., "Inter-Disciplinary Cooperative Investigations at Big Bone Lick State Park, Northern Kentucky," *Geological Society of America Abstracts with Programs* 37, no. 5 (2005): 14; Frank R. Ettensohn, "The Pre-Illinoian Lake Clays of the Cincinnati Region," *Ohio Journal of Science* 74 (1974): 215; W. C. Swadley, "The Preglacial Kentucky River of Northern Kentucky," in *Geological Survey Research 1971: U.S. Geological Survey Professional Paper 750-D* (1971), D127–D130; Deidre M. McCartney, Megan A.

Finney, and J. Barry Maynard, "Sources of the Salt in the Big Bone Lick Springs, Northern Kentucky," *Geological Society of America Abstracts with Programs* 37, no. 5 (2005): 34.

7. Potter, *Exploring the Geology*, 13–16; James T. Teller and Richard P. Goldthwait, "The Old Kentucky River; A Major Tributary to the Teays River," in "Geology and Hydrogeology of the Teays-Mahomet Bedrock Valley System," ed. W. N. Melhorn and J. P. Kempton, *Geological Society of America Special Paper 258* (1991), 29–31.

8. Richard H. Durrell, *A Recycled Landscape* (Cincinnati: Cincinnati Museum of Natural History, 1995), 3.

9. Swadley, "The Preglacial Kentucky River," D131.

10. Louis L. Ray, "Geomorphology and Quaternary Geology of the Glaciated Ohio River Valley—A Reconnaissance Study," *U.S. Geological Survey Professional Paper 826* (1974), 70.

11. Durrell, *A Recycled Landscape*, 8.

12. Ray, "Geomorphology," 70–71.

13. Tankersley, "Potential for Early-Man Sites at Big Bone Lick," 41, 44; Johnson and Andrews, "Inter-Disciplinary Cooperative Investigations at Big Bone Lick," 14; Nathaniel S. Shaler, "Appendix II: On the Age of the Bison in the Ohio Valley," in Joel A. Allen, "The American Bisons, Living and Extinct," *Memoirs, Museum of Comparative Zoology at Harvard College* 4, no. 10 (1876): 233.

2. Source of Salt and Health

1. Mark Kurlansky, *Salt: A World History* (New York: Walker, 2002), 6, 9; Ian W. Brown, *Salt and the Eastern North American Indian: An Archaeological Study*, Lower Mississippi Survey Bulletin, no. 6 (Cambridge, Mass.: Peabody Museum, Harvard University, 1980), 3.

2. Gloria J. Wentowski, "Salt as an Ecological Factor in the Prehistory of Eastern United States" (master's thesis, University of North Carolina, 1970), 11, 19, 51, 53.

3. John Ingles, *Escape from Indian Captivity*, ed. Roberta I. Steele and Andrew L. Ingles (Radford, Va.: Steele, 1982), 8–39.

4. Wentowski, "Salt as an Ecological Factor," 18; James B. Griffin, *The Fort Ancient Aspect* (Ann Arbor: University of Michigan Press, 1943), 131; Howard A. MacCord, "The Bintz Site," *American Antiquity* 18, no. 3 (1953): 239–44; A. Gwynn Henderson, *The Prehistoric Farm-*

ers of Boone County, Kentucky (Lexington: Kentucky Archaeological Survey, 2006), 43; William H. Lowthert IV, "Resource Use and Settlement Patterning around the Saline Springs and Salt Licks in Big Bone Lick State Park, Boone County, Kentucky" (master's thesis, University of Kentucky, 1998), 60–62, 172–73.

5. Kurlansky, *Salt,* 10.

6. Brown, *Salt and the Eastern North American Indian,* 5; Wentowski, "Salt as an Ecological Factor," 50; Thomas D. Clark, "Salt, a Factor in the Settlement of Kentucky," *Filson Club History Quarterly* 12 (1938): 45.

7. Willard R. Jillson, *Big Bone Lick* (Louisville, Ky.: Standard Printing, 1936), 78–83, 89–91; Lucien V. Rule, "Jon D. Shane's Interview with Ephraim Sandusky," *Filson Club History Quarterly* 8 (1934): 221.

8. Jennifer S. Warner, *Boone County: From Mastodons to the Millennium* (Burlington, Ky.: Boone County Bicentennial Books, 1998), 40; Humphrey Marshall, *The History of Kentucky* (Frankfort, Ky.: Gore, 1812), 405–6; Clark, "Salt," 43; Isaac Lippincott, "The Early Salt Trade of the Ohio Valley," *Journal of Political Economy* 20, no. 10 (1912): 1039.

9. Jillson, *Big Bone Lick,* 42, 84; Zadok Cramer, *The Navigator,* 7th ed. (Pittsburgh: Cramer, Spear, and Eichbaum, 1811), in Jillson, *Big Bone Lick,* 92–93.

10. Thomas Ashe, *Travels in America, Performed in 1806* (Pittsburgh: Cramer and Spear, 1808), 233; Lewis Collins, *Historical Sketches of Kentucky* (Maysville, Ky.: Collins, 1848), 181; Lippincott, "The Early Salt Trade," 1046; John A. Jakle, "Salt on the Ohio Valley Frontier, 1770–1820," *Annals of the Association of American Geographers* 59, no. 4 (1969): 700.

11. Letter from William Clark to Thomas Jefferson, November 10, 1807, in Howard C. Rice Jr., "Jefferson's Gift of Fossils to the Museum of Natural History in Paris," *Proceedings of the American Philosophical Society* 95 (1951): 602.

12. John Filson, *The Discovery, Settlement, and Present State of Kentucke* (Wilmington, Del.: Adams, 1784), 33; Jillson, *Big Bone Lick,* 94–96; Constantine S. Rafinesque, "Visit to Big-Bone Lick, in 1821," *Monthly American Journal of Geology and Natural Science* 1 (1832): 357; Cramer, *The Navigator,* 93.

13. Daniel Drake, *Natural and Statistical View, or Picture of Cincin-*

nati and the Miami Country (Cincinnati: Looker and Wallace, 1815), 195–96.

14. Daniel Drake, "Notice of the Principal Mineral Springs of Kentucky and Ohio," *Western Journal of the Medical and Physical Sciences* 2, no. 3 (1828): 161–62; J. Winston Coleman, *Springs of Kentucky* (Lexington, Ky.: Winburn Press, 1955), 16–17.

15. "Boone and the Big Bone Springs," *Licking Valley Register,* March 13, 1847; Collins, *Historical Sketches,* 181; "The Big Bone Springs, Boone County, Kentucky," *Cincinnati Daily Enquirer,* June 23, 1866; William Conrad, ed., *Boone County: The Top of Kentucky, 1792–1992* (Fort Mitchell, Ky.: Picture This! Books, 1992), 20–21; Lewis Collins and Richard H. Collins, *History of Kentucky* (Covington, Ky.: Collins, 1874), 1:191–92, 2:52.

16. "Local News," *Boone County Recorder,* May 25, 1876; S. E. J., "Clay House, Big Bone Springs, Ky.," *Covington Ticket,* August 29, 1876.

17. "Big Bone Springs," *Covington Daily Commonwealth,* April 26, 1881.

18. B. N. Griffing, *An Atlas of Boone, Kenton and Campbell Counties, Kentucky* (Philadelphia: D. J. Lake, 1883), 22.

19. Myrax J. Crouch, "Big Bone Springs," *Boone County Recorder,* December 26, 1894.

20. Coleman, *Springs of Kentucky,* 94–95; "Local News," *Boone County Recorder,* September 30, 1908; "New Company Would Place Big Bone, Ky., 'On the Map,'" *Kentucky Post (Covington),* February 28, 1916; John R. Branch, "The Geomorphology and Pleistocene Geology of the Big Bone Lick Area of Kentucky" (master's thesis, University of Cincinnati, 1946), 9; Betty Jo Roter, *White Kittens and Four-Leaf Clovers* (Mt. Vernon, Ind.: Windmill, 1997), 237–39.

3. Indian Accounts of Great Buffalo

1. Benjamin S. Barton, *Archaeologiae Americanae Telluris Collectanea et Specimena* (Philadelphia: Barton, 1814), 34; letter from James Wright to John Bartram, August 22, 1762, in George G. Simpson, "The Beginnings of Vertebrate Paleontology in North America," *Proceedings of the American Philosophical Society* 86, no. 1 (1942): 140–41.

2. John A. Jakle, "Salt on the Ohio Valley Frontier, 1770–1820," *Annals of the Association of American Geographers* 59, no. 4 (1969): 688–

691; Lewis Collins, *Historical Sketches of Kentucky* (Maysville, Ky.: Collins, 1848), 181.

3. George W. Featherstonehaugh, ed., "The Journal of Col. Croghan," *Monthly American Journal of Geology and Natural Science* 1 (1831): 262; William E. Myer, "Indian Trails of the Southeast," in *U.S. Bureau of American Ethnology, 42nd Annual Report* (Washington, D.C., 1928), 788–90, 793; Kenneth B. Tankersley, "Bison Exploitation by Late Fort Ancient Peoples in the Central Ohio River Valley," *North American Archaeologist* 7, no. 4 (1986): 295.

4. Wright to Bartram, 140; *hoppisses* in the original letter was mistakenly copied as *Noppusses* in the transcription.

5. Adrienne Mayor, *Fossil Legends of the First Americans* (Princeton, N.J.: Princeton University Press, 2005), 30, 41–43; Erminnie A. Smith, "Myths of the Iroquois," in *Second Annual Report of the Bureau of American Ethnology, 1880–1881* (Washington, D.C., 1883), 51.

6. Charles A. Hanna, *The Wilderness Trail* (New York: Putnam's, 1911), 2:39–42; Whitfield J. Bell Jr., "A Box of Old Bones: A Note on the Identification of the Mastodon, 1766–1806," *Proceedings of the American Philosophical Society* 93, no. 2 (1949): 169–71.

7. Indian narrative in William Winterbotham, *An Historical, Geographical, Commercial, and Philosophical View of the United States of America* (New York: Reid, 1796), 3:140.

8. Mayor, *Fossil Legends*, 24–25.

9. Letter from Peter Collinson to John Bartram, June 11, 1762, in *The Correspondence of John Bartram, 1734–1777*, ed. Edmund Berkeley and Dorothy S. Berkeley (Gainesville: University Press of Florida, 1992), 562–63.

10. Thomas Jefferson, *Notes on the State of Virginia* (London: Stockdale, 1787; reprint, Chapel Hill: University of North Carolina Press, 1955), 43.

11. Smith, "Myths of the Iroquois," 65–66.

12. Charles M. Barbeau, *Mythologie huronne et wyandotte* (Montreal: University of Montreal Press, 1994), 276–78; Mayor, *Fossil Legends*, 28–29; Smith, "Myths of the Iroquois," 66–67; William M. Beauchamp, *Iroquois Folk Lore* (Syracuse, N.Y.: Dehler, 1922), 41–51.

13. Nicholas Cresswell, *The Journal of Nicholas Cresswell, 1774–1777* (New York: Dial, 1928), 87–89.

4. Gathering the Bones

1. Reuben G. Thwaites, *Afloat on the Ohio* (Chicago: Way and Williams, 1897), 299–306.

2. George G. Simpson, "The Discovery of Fossil Vertebrates in North America," *Journal of Paleontology* 17, no. 1 (1943): 28–29, 34; Sylvester K. Stevens and Donald H. Kent, *The Expedition of Baron de Longueuil* (Harrisburg, Pa.: Erie County Historical Society, 1941), 2–4.

3. Stevens and Kent, *Expedition of Longueuil,* 4–7.

4. Letter from Jean-Bernard Bossu to the Marquis de l'Estrade, November 10, 1756, in *Jean-Bernard Bossu's Travels in the Interior of North America, 1751–1762,* ed. Seymour Feiler (Norman: University of Oklahoma Press, 1962), ix, 103–12; B. F. French, ed., *Historical Collections of Louisiana* (Philadelphia: Daniels and Smith, 1850), 2:83.

5. Jean-Étienne Guettard, "Mémoire dans lequel on compare le Canada à la Suisse, par rapport à ses minéraux," *Histoire de l'Académie royale des Sciences, Année 1752* (Paris, 1756), 189–220; Pascal Tassy, "The Emergence of the Concept of Fossil Species: The American Mastodon (Proboscidea, Mammalia), a History between Clarity and Confusion," *Geodiversitas* 24, no. 2 (2002): 266–69; George G. Simpson, "The Beginnings of Vertebrate Paleontology in North America," *Proceedings of the American Philosophical Society* 86, no. 1 (1942): 144; Claudine Cohen, *The Fate of the Mammoth* (Chicago: University of Chicago Press, 2002), 90.

6. Louis J. M. Daubenton, "Mémoire sur des os et des dents remarquables par leur grandeur," *Histoire de l'Académie royale des Sciences, Année 1762* (Paris, 1764), 206–29; Paul Semonin, *American Monster* (New York: New York University Press, 2000), 62–83.

7. Simpson, "Beginnings of Vertebrate Paleontology," 145.

8. Rembrandt Peale, *An Historical Disquisition on the Mammoth* (London: Lawrence, 1803), 11; Georges L. Leclerc de Buffon, *Historie naturelle, générale et particulière IX* (Paris: Imprimeries royale, 1761), 126.

9. Cohen, *Fate of the Mammoth,* 98; Georges L. Leclerc de Buffon, *Historie naturelle, générale et particulière XI* (Paris: Imprimeries royale, 1764), 86.

10. Georges-Louis Leclerc de Buffon, *Les Époques de la nature* (Paris, 1778), in *Natural History, General and Particular, by the Count de Buf-*

fon, 3rd ed., ed. and trans. William Smellie (London: Strahan, 1791), 299; William M. Darlington, ed., *Christopher Gist's Journals* (Pittsburgh: Weldon, 1893), 57–58.

11. Lucien Beckner, "John Findley: The First Pathfinder of Kentucky," *History Quarterly of the Filson Club* 1, no. 3 (1927): 113; John Ingles, *Escape from Indian Captivity*, ed. Roberta I. Steele and Andrew L. Ingles (Radford, Va.: Steele, 1982), 12.

12. Semonin, *American Monster*, 97; Thwaites, *Afloat on the Ohio*, 307, 312–13.

13. James Kenny, "Journal of James Kenny, 1761–1763," ed. John W. Jordan, *Pennsylvania Magazine of History and Biography* 37, no. 1 (1913): 1, 42–43, 163, 180.

14. Alfred A. Cave, "George Croghan and the Emergence of British Influence on the Ohio Frontier," in *Builders of Ohio*, ed. Warren Van Tine and Michael Pierce (Columbus: Ohio State University Press, 2003), 1, 5; letter from Peter Collinson to John Bartram, June 11, 1762, in *The Correspondence of John Bartram, 1734–1777*, ed. Edmund Berkeley and Dorothy S. Berkeley (Gainesville: University Press of Florida, 1992), 562–63.

15. Letter from Peter Collinson to John Bartram, July 25, 1762, in *Correspondence of Bartram*, 565–66.

16. Letter from John Bartram to Peter Collinson, December 3, 1762, in ibid., 579–80.

17. Letter from Peter Collinson to John Bartram, December 10, 1762, and letter from John Bartram to Peter Collinson, May 1, 1763, in ibid., 580–82, 590–91.

18. Nicholas B. Wainwright, *George Croghan: Wilderness Diplomat* (Chapel Hill: University of North Carolina Press, 1959), 219–23; George W. Featherstonehaugh, ed., "The Journal of Col. Croghan," *Monthly American Journal of Geology and Natural Science* 1 (1831): 261–64.

19. Wainwright, *George Croghan*, 233–34; Harry Gordon, "Journal of an Expedition along the Ohio and Mississippi by Captain Harry Gordon," in Edward M. Kindle, "The Story of the Discovery of Big Bone Lick," *Kentucky Geological Survey*, 6th ser., 41 (1931): 199–200.

20. Whitfield J. Bell Jr., "A Box of Old Bones: A Note on the Identification of the Mastodon, 1766–1806," *Proceedings of the American Philosophical Society* 93, no. 2 (1949): 170–71, 176.

5. Animal Incognitum

1. Nicholas B. Wainwright, *George Croghan: Wilderness Diplomat* (Chapel Hill: University of North Carolina Press, 1959), 239–41; Paul Semonin, *American Monster* (New York: New York University Press, 2000), 109–10.

2. Letter from George Croghan to the Earl of Shelburne, January 16, 1767, in Edward M. Kindle, "The Story of the Discovery of Big Bone Lick," *Kentucky Geological Survey*, 6th ser., 41 (1931): 201; Peter Collinson, "An Account of Some Very Large Fossil Teeth, Found in North America, and Described by Peter Collinson, F. R. S.," *Philosophical Transactions* 57 (1767): 467; Semonin, *American Monster*, 108.

3. Wainwright, *George Croghan*, 239–40; Collinson, "An Account," 467; letter from Benjamin Franklin to George Croghan, August 5, 1767, in Kindle, "Discovery of Big Bone Lick," 202–3.

4. Letter from Peter Collinson to John Bartram, September 19, 1767, in *The Correspondence of John Bartram, 1734–1777*, ed. Edmund Berkeley and Dorothy S. Berkeley (Gainesville: University Press of Florida, 1992), 688–89.

5. Claudine Cohen, *The Fate of the Mammoth* (Chicago: University of Chicago Press, 2002), 70–73; Collinson, "An Account," 465–66.

6. Peter Collinson, "Sequel to the Foregoing Account of the Large Fossil Teeth," *Philosophical Transactions* 57 (1767): 468–69.

7. Letter from Benjamin Franklin to Abbé Chappe, January 31, 1768, in Kindle, "Discovery of Big Bone Lick," 203–4.

8. Pascal Tassy, "The Emergence of the Concept of Fossil Species: The American Mastodon (Proboscidea, Mammalia), a History between Clarity and Confusion," *Geodiversitas* 24, no. 2 (2002): 283–86; letter from Peter Collinson to Georges-Louis Leclerc de Buffon, July 3, 1767, quoted in Rembrandt Peale, *An Historical Disquisition on the Mammoth* (London: Lawrence, 1803), 13.

9. Georges-Louis Leclerc de Buffon, *Historie naturelle, générale et particuliè IX* (Paris: Imprimeries royale, 1761), 126; letter from Peter Collinson to John Bartram, May 17, 1768, in *Correspondence of Bartram*, 701–3; Collinson, "Sequel," 469.

10. William Hunter, "Observations on the Bones, Commonly Supposed to Be Elephants Bones, Which Have Been Found Near the River Ohio in America," *Philosophical Transactions* 58 (1768): 34–45.

11. Thomas Hutchins, *Journey from Fort Pitt to the Mouth of the*

Ohio, in *Documents Relating to the French Settlements on the Wabash*, ed. Jacob P. Dunn (Indianapolis: Indiana Historical Society, 1894), 2:419.

12. Lyman C. Draper, *The Life of Daniel Boone*, ed. Ted F. Belue (Mechanicsburg, Pa.: Stackpole, 1998), 244; Lewis Collins and Richard H. Collins, *History of Kentucky* (Covington, Ky.: Collins, 1874), 2:55, 606–7; Robert McAfee, *Journal of an Exploration through Kentucky in 1773*, in Willard R. Jillson, *Big Bone Lick* (Louisville, Ky.: Standard Printing, 1936), 20–21; Humphrey Marshall, *The History of Kentucky* (Frankfort, Ky.: Gore, 1812), 86.

13. John Floyd, *Survey of Big Bone Lick, May 12, 1774*, in Jillson, *Big Bone Lick*, 76; Thomas Hanson, *Journal Kept on the River Ohio in the Year 1774*, in *Documentary History of Dunmore's War 1774*, ed. Reuben G. Thwaites and Louise P. Kellogg (Madison: Wisconsin Historical Society, 1905), 121.

14. Nicholas Cresswell, *The Journal of Nicholas Cresswell, 1774–1777* (New York: Dial, 1928), 87–88.

15. Thomas Hutchins, *A New Map of the Western Parts of Virginia, Pennsylvania, Maryland, and North Carolina* (London: Almon, 1778; reprint, Cleveland: Clark, 1904); Thomas Hutchins, *A Topographical Description of Virginia, Pennsylvania, Maryland, and North Carolina* (London: Almon, 1778; reprint, Cleveland: Clark, 1904), 82–83.

16. Thomas Pennant, *Synopsis of Quadrupeds* (Chester, U.K.: Monk, 1771), 92; Oliver Goldsmith, *An History of the Earth and Animated Nature* (London: Nourse, 1774), 4:283–84; Semonin, *American Monster*, 157–60.

17. Whitfield J. Bell Jr., "A Box of Old Bones: A Note on the Identification of the Mastodon, 1766–1806," *Proceedings of the American Philosophical Society* 93, no. 2 (1949): 174; Georges Cuvier, *Researches on Fossil Bones* (London: Henderson, 1835), 323.

18. Cohen, *Fate of the Mammoth*, 95; Georges-Louis Leclerc de Buffon, *Les Époques de la nature* (Paris, 1778; reprint, Paris: Muséum National d'Histoire Naturelle, 1962), 223–28; Peale, *An Historical Disquisition*, 14–15.

6. Thomas Jefferson Takes an Interest

1. Robert Annan, "Account of a Skeleton of a Large Animal, Found Near Hudson's River," *Memoirs of the American Academy of Arts and Sciences* 2, pt. 1 (1793): 160–64.

2. Paul Semonin, *American Monster* (New York: New York University Press, 2000), 175–78; Annan, "Account of a Skeleton," 164; Humphreys quoted in Ezra Stiles diary, February 17, 1781, in *The Literary Diary of Ezra Stiles*, ed. Franklin B. Dexter (New York: Scribner's, 1901), 2:511.

3. Edward Taylor diary, July 23, 1705, in *Extracts from the Itineraries and Other Miscellanies of Ezra Stiles, D.D., LL.D., 1755–1794*, ed. Franklin B. Dexter (New Haven, Conn.: Yale University Press, 1916), 82; letter from Edward Hyde to the Secretary of the Royal Society, undated, in Charles R. Weld, *A History of the Royal Society* (London: Parker, 1848), 1:421–22.

4. Taylor diary, June 1706, in *Extracts and Itineraries of Stiles*, 82; Semonin, *American Monster*, 25; letter from Joseph Dudley to Cotton Mather, July 10, 1706, in Donald E. Stanford, "The Giant Bones of Claverack, New York, 1705, Described by the Colonial Poet, Reverend Edward Taylor (ca. 1642–1729) in a Manuscript Owned by Yale University Library," *New York History* 40 (1959): 49–50.

5. Dexter, *Extracts and Itineraries of Stiles*, 206; Taylor diary, June 1706, in ibid., 82.

6. Thomas H. Johnson, *The Poetical Works of Edward Taylor* (Princeton, N.J.: Princeton University Press, 1943), 221, 224; Dexter, *Extracts and Itineraries of Stiles*, 83.

7. Letter from Ezra Stiles to Thomas Jefferson, June 21, 1784, in *The Papers of Thomas Jefferson*, ed. Julian P. Boyd (Princeton, N.J.: Princeton University Press, 1952–1956), 7:313–15; Dexter, *Extracts and Itineraries of Stiles*, 86; Stiles diary, August 25, 1777, in *Literary Diary of Stiles*, 2:201; Edmund S. Morgan, *A Gentle Puritan: A Life of Ezra Stiles, 1725–1795* (New York: Norton, 1983), 97, 114, 290, 308.

8. Stiles diary, June 8, 1784, in *Literary Diary of Stiles*, 3:124–26; letter from Thomas Jefferson to Ezra Stiles, June 10, 1784, in *Papers of Jefferson*, 7:304–5.

9. Letter from Ezra Stiles to Thomas Jefferson, June 21, 1784, in *Papers of Jefferson*, 7:312–17.

10. Letter from Thomas Jefferson to Ezra Stiles, July 17, 1785, in ibid., 8:298–300.

11. Stiles diary, April 26, 1786, in *Literary Diary of Stiles*, 2:214–15; letter from Ezra Stiles to Thomas Jefferson, May 8, 1786, in *Papers of Jefferson*, 9:476–77.

12. Thomas Jefferson, *Notes on the State of Virginia* (London: Stockdale, 1787; reprint, Chapel Hill: University of North Carolina Press, 1955), xii–xix.

13. Ibid., 43, 53–54.

14. Ibid., 44–46.

15. Ibid., 47–53, 268.

16. Semonin, *American Monster,* 270–76.

17. Letter from Thomas Jefferson to George Rogers Clark, December 19, 1781, in *Papers of Jefferson,* 6:139; Samuel W. Thomas and Eugene H. Conner, "George Rogers Clark (1752–1818): Natural Scientist and Historian," *Filson Club History Quarterly* 41 (1967): 214.

18. Letter from George R. Clark to Thomas Jefferson, February 20, 1782, in *Papers of Jefferson,* 6:159–60.

19. Letters from Thomas Jefferson to George Rogers Clark, November 26, 1782, and January 6, 1783, in ibid., 6:204–5, 218–19.

20. Letter from George R. Clark to Thomas Jefferson, October 12, 1783, in Thomas and Conner, "George Rogers Clark," 218.

21. Letter from Thomas Jefferson to George Rogers Clark, December 4, 1783, in *Papers of Jefferson,* 6:371; letter from George R. Clark to Thomas Jefferson, February 8, 1784, in Thomas and Conner, "George Rogers Clark," 218; letter from Thomas Jefferson to Benjamin Smith Barton, February 27, 1803, in *Letters of the Lewis and Clark Expedition,* ed. Donald Jackson (Urbana: University of Illinois Press, 1978), 1:16–17.

22. Stiles diary, June 8, 1784, in *Literary Diary of Stiles,* 3:126; letters from Arthur Campbell to Thomas Jefferson, November 7, 1782, and November 29, 1782, in *Papers of Jefferson,* 6:201, 208.

7. *A Question of Tusks*

1. Whitfield J. Bell Jr., "A Box of Old Bones: A Note on the Identification of the Mastodon, 1766–1806," *Proceedings of the American Philosophical Society* 93, no. 2 (1949): 171–72; Robert Annan, "Account of a Skeleton of a Large Animal, Found Near Hudson's River," *Memoirs of the American Academy of Arts and Sciences* 2, pt. 1 (1793): 160–64.

2. Bell, "A Box of Old Bones," 172–73; Charles C. Sellers, *Charles Willson Peale* (New York: Scribner's, 1969), 202–4, 460.

3. Bell, "A Box of Old Bones," 173–75; letter from Petrus Camper to John Morgan, July 28, 1787, in Bell, "A Box of Old Bones," 175;

Robert P. W. Visser, *The Zoological Work of Petrus Camper (1722–1789)* (Amsterdam: Rodopi, 1985), 125–26.

4. John Walton, *John Filson of Kentucke* (Lexington: University of Kentucky Press, 1956), 17–24; John Filson, *This Map of Kentucke, etc.* (Philadelphia: Rook, 1784); John Filson, *The Discovery, Settlement, and Present State of Kentucke* (Wilmington, Del.: Adams, 1784), 34–35.

5. Filson, *Discovery, Settlement, and Present State,* 35–36.

6. Paul Semonin, *American Monster* (New York: New York University Press, 2000), 186; Henry Phillips Jr., "Early Proceedings of the American Philosophical Society," *Proceedings of the American Philosophical Society* 22, no. 119 (1885): 123; "Description of Bones, &c. Found near the River Ohio," *Columbian Magazine* 1 (1786): 106.

7. Ebenezer Denny, *Military Journal of Major Ebenezer Denny* (Philadelphia: Historical Society of Philadelphia, 1859), 60.

8. Semonin, *American Monster,* 211; letter from Samuel H. Parsons to Ezra Stiles, April 27, 1786, in *The Papers of Thomas Jefferson,* ed. Julian P. Boyd (Princeton, N.J.: Princeton University Press, 1952–1956), 13:477–78.

9. Samuel H. Parsons, "Discoveries Made in the Western Country," *Memoirs of the American Academy of Arts and Sciences* 1, pt. 2 (1793): 122–23.

10. Nicholas Collin, "An Essay on Those Inquiries in Natural Philosophy, Which at Present Are Most Beneficial to the United States of North America," *Transactions of the American Philosophical Society* 3 (1793): xxiv; Charles W. Peale, "Broadside: My Design in Forming This Museum," in *The Selected Papers of Charles Willson Peale and His Family,* ed. Lillian B. Miller (New Haven, Conn.: Yale University Press, 1983–1996), 2(1):15–16.

11. Charles Kerr, ed., *History of Kentucky* (Chicago: American Historical Society, 1922), 1:532; James Taylor, "Autobiography," in J. Stoddard Johnston, *First Explorations of Kentucky* (Louisville, Ky.: Morton, 1898), 170.

12. Gardiner Baker, "Broadside: Museum & Wax-Work, at the Exchange, New-York," in Robert M. McClung and Gale S. McClung, "Tammany's Remarkable Gardiner Baker," *New York Historical Society Quarterly* 43 (1958): 142; James Smith, "Journey through Kentucky and into the Northwest Territory, 1795," *Ohio Archaeological and Historical Publications* 16 (1907): 383; William Cooper, "Notices of Big-

Bone Lick," *Monthly American Journal of Geology and Natural Science* 1 (1831): 161; Oliver P. Hay, *The Pleistocene of North America and Its Vertebrated Animals from the States East of the Mississippi River and from the Canadian Provinces East of Longitude 95°* (Washington, D.C.: Carnegie Institution of Washington, 1923), 401.

13. Letter from Étienne G. Saint-Hilaire and Jean-Baptiste Lamarck to Charles Willson Peale, January 30, 1796, in *Selected Papers of Peale*, 2(1):142; Martin J. S. Rudwick, *Georges Cuvier, Fossil Bones, and Geological Catastrophes* (Chicago: University of Chicago Press, 1997), 15–16.

14. Georges Cuvier, *Researches on Fossil Bones*, 4th rev. ed. (London: Henderson, 1835), 323–24.

15. Georges Cuvier, "Mémoire sur les espèces, d'éléphans, tant vivantes que fossiles," *Magasin encyclopédique* 3 (1796): 440–45, trans. and reprinted in Rudwick, *Georges Cuvier*, 18–24.

16. George Turner, "Memoir on the Extraneous Fossils, Denominated Mammoth Bones," *Transactions of the American Philosophical Society* 4 (1799): 510–18; George G. Simpson, "The Beginnings of Vertebrate Paleontology in North America," *Proceedings of the American Philosophical Society* 86, no. 1 (1942): 151.

8. William Goforth's Stolen Specimens

1. George Turner, "Memoir on the Extraneous Fossils, Denominated Mammoth Bones," *Transactions of the American Philosophical Society* 4 (1799): 515; Henry Phillips Jr., "Early Proceedings of the American Philosophical Society," *Proceedings of the American Philosophical Society* 22, no. 119 (1885): 258; American Philosophical Society circular (1799), in Silvio A. Bedini, *Thomas Jefferson: Statesman of Science* (New York: Macmillan, 1990), 280–81; John C. Greene, *The Death of Adam* (Ames: Iowa State University Press, 1959), 109.

2. Rembrandt Peale, *An Historical Disquisition on the Mammoth* (London: Lawrence, 1803), 17–20.

3. Letter from Thomas Jefferson to Robert R. Livingston, December 14, 1800, in *The Writings of Thomas Jefferson*, ed. Albert E. Bergh (Washington, D.C.: Thomas Jefferson Memorial Association, 1907), 10:176–80; letter from Thomas Jefferson to Caspar Wistar, February 3, 1801, in Henry F. Osborn, "Thomas Jefferson as a Paleontologist," *Science* 82 (1935): 535; Peale, *An Historical Disquisition*,

21–22; letter from Charles W. Peale to Elizabeth DePeyster Peale, June 28, 1801, in *The Selected Papers of Charles Willson Peale and His Family*, ed. Lillian B. Miller (New Haven, Conn.: Yale University Press, 1983–1996), 2(1):336.

4. Peale, *An Historical Disquisition*, 24–34.

5. George G. Simpson, "The Beginnings of Vertebrate Paleontology in North America," *Proceedings of the American Philosophical Society* 86 (1942): 159; Peale, *An Historical Disquisition*, 34–36, 60.

6. Greene, *The Death of Adam*, 113–14; Peale, *An Historical Disquisition*, 75–79.

7. Peale, *An Historical Disquisition*, 51–53; John D. Godman, *American Natural History* (Philadelphia: Carey and Lea, 1826), 230.

8. Peale, *An Historical Disquisition*, 68, 90.

9. Ibid., 90; Thomas Jefferson, "A Memoir on the Discovery of Certain Bones of a Quadruped of the Clawed Kind in the Western Parts of Virginia," *Transactions of the American Philosophical Society* 4 (1799): 246–60; Caspar Wistar, "A Description of the Bones Deposited, by the President, in the Museum of the Society, and Represented in the Annexed Plates," *Transactions of the American Philosophical Society* 4 (1799): 526–31.

10. Peale, *An Historical Disquisition*, 84–85, 90; Rembrandt Peale, "Account of Some Remains of a Species of Gigantic Oxen Found in America and Other Parts of the World," *Philosophical Magazine* 15 (1803): 325–27.

11. Peale, *An Historical Disquisition*, 90–91.

12. Jefferson, "A Memoir," 255–56.

13. Ibid., 252.

14. Letter from Thomas Jefferson to Bernard Lacépède, February 24, 1803, in *Letters of the Lewis and Clark Expedition*, ed. Donald Jackson (Urbana: University of Illinois Press, 1978), 1:15.

15. Letter from Charles W. Peale to Thomas Jefferson, July 18, 1803, in ibid., 132.

16. Letter from Meriwether Lewis to Thomas Jefferson, October 3, 1803, in ibid., 127, 130.

17. Letter from Gideon Fitz to Thomas Jefferson, October 19, 1804, in ibid., 132.

18. Letter from Caspar Wistar to William Goforth, December 1, 1806, in Willard R. Jillson, *Big Bone Lick* (Louisville, Ky.: Standard Printing, 1936), 39.

19. Letter from William Goforth to Thomas Jefferson, [1807?], in ibid., 40–43.

20. Zadok Cramer, *The Navigator*, 8th ed. (Pittsburgh: Cramer, Spear, and Eichbaum, 1814), 201–4, in Jillson, *Big Bone Lick*, 37–38.

21. Thomas Ashe, *Memoirs and Confessions of Captain Ashe, Author of "The Spirit of the Book," &c. &c. &c.* (London: Colburn, 1815), 2:215; Thomas Ashe, *Memoirs of Mammoth, and Various Other Extraordinary and Stupendous Bones, of Incognita, or Non-Descript Animals, Found in the Vicinity of the Ohio, Wabash, Illinois, Mississippi, Missouri, Osage, and Red Rivers, &c. &c.* (Liverpool: Harris, 1806), 6–12, 18, 24.

22. Ashe, *Memoirs of Mammoth*, 7–60.

23. Daniel Drake, "Notice of the Principal Mineral Springs of Kentucky and Ohio," *Western Journal of the Medical and Physical Sciences* 2, no. 3 (1828): 159; William Cooper, "Notices of Big-Bone Lick," *Monthly American Journal of Geology and Natural Science* 1 (1831): 160–62, 171.

9. William Clark's Bountiful Collection

1. Georges Cuvier, *Extract from a Work on the Species of Quadrupeds of Which the Bones Have Been Found in the Interior of the Earth* (Paris, 1800), in Martin J. S. Rudwick, *Georges Cuvier, Fossil Bones, and Geological Catastrophes* (Chicago: University of Chicago Press, 1997), 53.

2. Georges Cuvier, "Sur le Grand Mastodonte," *Annales du Muséum d'Histoire naturelle* 8 (1806): 270–312.

3. Letter from Benjamin S. Barton to Bernard Lacépède, 1805, in Georges Cuvier, *Researches on Fossil Bones* (London: Henderson, 1835), 277–78.

4. Cuvier, "Grand Mastodonte," 270–312; Georges Cuvier, *Researches on the Fossil Bones of Quadrupeds* (Paris, 1812), 2:42, in Claudine Cohen, *The Fate of the Mammoth* (Chicago: University of Chicago Press, 2002), 100.

5. Letter from Thomas Jefferson to Caspar Wistar, February 25, 1807, in *The Writings of Thomas Jefferson*, ed. Albert E. Bergh (Washington, D.C.: Thomas Jefferson Memorial Association, 1907), 11:158–59.

6. Letter from William Clark to Jonathan Clark, September 9, 1807, in *Dear Brother: Letters of William Clark to Jonathan Clark*, ed. James J. Holmberg (New Haven, Conn.: Yale University Press, 2002), 126; letter from William Clark to Thomas Jefferson, September 20, 1807, in Howard C. Rice Jr., "Jefferson's Gift of Fossils to the Museum

of Natural History in Paris," *Proceedings of the American Philosophical Society* 95 (1951): 600.

7. Letter from William Clark to Thomas Jefferson, November 10, 1807, in Rice, "Jefferson's Gift," 600–604.

8. Ibid.

9. Rice, "Jefferson's Gift," 598, 603–4; letter from Thomas Jefferson to Caspar Wistar, December 19, 1807, in *Writings of Jefferson*, 11:403–4.

10. Letter from Thomas Jefferson to William Clark, December 19, 1807, in Rice, "Jefferson's Gift," 604.

11. Letter from Thomas Jefferson to William Clark, September 10, 1809, in *Writings of Jefferson*, 12:309–11; letter from Thomas Jefferson to Caspar Wistar, March 8, 1808, in Rice, "Jefferson's Gift," 605; Silvio A. Bedini, *Thomas Jefferson and American Vertebrate Paleontology* (Charlottesville: Virginia Division of Mineral Resources, 1985), 12.

12. Rice, "Jefferson's Gift," 609–11, 615–17.

13. Letter from Thomas Jefferson to Charles Willson Peale, May 5, 1809, in *The Papers of Thomas Jefferson: Retirement Series*, ed. J. Jefferson Looney (Princeton, N.J.: Princeton University Press, 2004), 187.

14. Letter from Thomas Jefferson to William Clark, September 10, 1809, in *Writings of Jefferson*, 12:309–11.

15. Letter from Thomas Jefferson to John Adams, April 11, 1823, in *The Adams-Jefferson Letters*, ed. Lester J. Cappon (New York: Simon and Schuster, 1971), 592.

16. Henry Phillips Jr., "Early Proceedings of the American Philosophical Society," *Proceedings of the American Philosophical Society* 22, no. 119 (1885): 413–14, 451, 478; Caspar Wistar, "An Account of Two Heads Found in the Morass, Called the Big Bone Lick, and Presented to the Society, by Mr. Jefferson," *Transactions of the American Philosophical Society*, n.s., 1 (1818): 375–80.

17. Wistar, "An Account of Two Heads," 377–79; letter from William Clark to Thomas Jefferson, November 10, 1807, in Rice, "Jefferson's Gift," 602; William B. Scott, "*Cervalces americanus*, a Fossil Moose, or Elk, from the Quaternary of New Jersey," *Proceedings of the Academy of Natural Sciences of Philadelphia* 37 (1885): 181–202.

18. Björn Kurtén and Elaine Anderson, *Pleistocene Mammals of North America* (New York: Columbia University Press, 1980), 317; Kenneth B. Tankersley, "Ice Age Giants," in Bradley T. Lepper, *Ohio Archaeology* (Wilmington, Ohio: Orange Frazer, 2005), 36.

19. Wistar, "An Account of Two Heads," 379–80.

20. Richard Harlan, *Fauna Americana* (Philadelphia: Finley, 1825), 271–72; Joseph Leidy, "Memoir on the Extinct Species of American Ox," *Smithsonian Contributions to Knowledge* 5, art. 3 (1852): 12, 17–19.

21. Kurtén and Anderson, *Pleistocene Mammals*, 332–34; Paul S. Martin and John E. Guilday, "A Bestiary for Pleistocene Biologists," in *Pleistocene Extinctions*, ed. P. S. Martin and H. E. Wright Jr. (New Haven, Conn.: Yale University Press, 1967), 57–58; Jerry N. McDonald and Clayton E. Ray, "The Autochthonous North American Musk Oxen *Bootherium, Symbos,* and *Gidleya* (Mammalia: Artiodactyla: Bovidae)," *Smithsonian Contributions to Paleobiology* 66 (1989): 67–68; R. Dale Guthrie, "New Paleoecological and Paleoethological Information on the Extinct Helmeted Muskoxen from Alaska," *Annales Zoologici Fennici* 28 (1992): 175–86.

22. Letter from William Clark to Thomas Jefferson, November 10, 1807, in Rice, "Jefferson's Gift," 602; Joseph Leidy, "[Remarks on Extinct Bison]," *Proceedings of the Academy of Natural Sciences of Philadelphia* 6 (1852): 117; Leidy, "Memoir on Extinct Species of American Ox," 11–12.

23. Kurtén and Anderson, *Pleistocene Mammals*, 337–38.

24. Oliver P. Hay, *The Pleistocene of North America and Its Vertebrated Animals from the States East of the Mississippi River and from the Canadian Provinces East of Longitude 95°* (Washington, D.C.: Carnegie Institution of Washington, 1923), 202; Kurtén and Anderson, *Pleistocene Mammals*, 290.

25. Kurtén and Anderson, *Pleistocene Mammals*, 290; Elaine Anderson, "Who's Who in the Pleistocene: A Mammalian Bestiary," in *Quaternary Extinctions*, ed. Paul S. Martin and Richard G. Klein (Tucson: University of Arizona Press, 1984), 65.

10. The Faunal List Evolves

1. Estwick Evans, *A Pedestrious Tour of Four Thousand Miles, through the Western States and Territories, during the Winter and Spring of 1818* (Concord, N.H.: Spear, 1819), in *Early Western Travels, 1748–1846*, ed. Reuben G. Thwaites (New York: AMS Press, 1966), 8:270–71.

2. Constantine S. Rafinesque, "Visit to Big Bone Lick, in 1821," *Monthly American Journal of Geology and Natural Science* 1 (1832): 356; Daniel Drake, "Notice of the Principal Mineral Springs of Kentucky and Ohio," *Western Journal of the Medical and Physical Sciences* 2, no. 3 (1828): 159.

3. William N. Blane, *An Excursion through the United States and Canada during the Years 1822–23* (London: Baldwin, Cradock, and Joy, 1824), 130, 133; Richard Harlan, *Fauna Americana* (Philadelphia: Finley, 1825), 223–25; Richard G. Wood, *Stephen Harriman Long, 1784–1864* (Glendale, Calif.: Clark, 1966), 139.

4. William Cooper, "Notices of Big-Bone Lick," *Monthly American Journal of Geology and Natural Science* 1 (1831): 163–64; Joseph Leidy, "Description of Vertebrate Fossils," in Francis S. Holmes, *Post-Pleiocene Fossils of South-Carolina* (Charleston, S.C.: Russell and Jones, 1858–1860), 107; Clayton E. Ray and Albert E. Sanders, "Pleistocene Tapirs in the Eastern United States," in *Contributions in Quaternary Vertebrate Paleontology*, ed. Hugh H. Genoways and Mary R. Dawson (Pittsburgh: Carnegie Museum of Natural History, 1984), 284, 288.

5. "Dr. Hays stated that the tooth of the fossil Tapir presented by him this evening, was found in the bed of a canal in North Carolina," *Proceedings of the Academy of Natural Sciences of Philadelphia* 6 (1852): 53; "Leidy proposed for it the name of *Tapirus Haysii*," *Proceedings of the Academy of Natural Sciences of Philadelphia* 6 (1852): 106; Leidy, "Description of Vertebrate Fossils," 106; Ray and Sanders, "Pleistocene Tapirs," 286, 288.

6. Drake, "Notice of the Principal Mineral Springs," 158, 159.

7. Frances Trollope, *Domestic Manners of the Americans*, ed. Donald Smalley (New York: Vintage Books, 1949), 141.

8. Cooper, "Notices of Big-Bone Lick," 163–64, 169, 171, 173–74; Oliver P. Hay, *The Pleistocene of North America and Its Vertebrated Animals from the States East of the Mississippi River and from the Canadian Provinces East of Longitude 95°* (Washington, D.C.: Carnegie Institution of Washington, 1923), 45.

9. Björn Kurtén and Elaine Anderson, *Pleistocene Mammals of North America* (New York: Columbia University Press, 1980), 137–38; Ian M. Lange, *Ice Age Mammals of North America* (Missoula, Mont.: Mountain Press, 2002), 82; Kenneth B. Tankersley, "Ice Age Giants," in Bradley T. Lepper, *Ohio Archaeology* (Wilmington, Ohio: Orange Frazer, 2005), 36.

10. Cooper, "Notices of Big-Bone Lick," 207; William D. Funkhouser and William S. Webb, *Ancient Life in Kentucky* (Frankfort: Kentucky Geological Survey, 1928), 42–43.

11. Cooper, "Notices of Big-Bone Lick," 159–60; Anonymous [lat-

er revealed to be Sayres Gazley], "Notice of the Osseous Remains at Big Bone Lick, Kentucky," *American Journal of Science* 18 (1830): 141; Charles Lyell, *Travels in North America* (New York: Wiley and Putnam, 1845), 2:55; Benjamin Silliman, "Remarks by the Editor," *American Journal of Science and Arts* 20 (1831): 371–72.

12. James Taylor, *Autobiography*, in J. Stoddard Johnston, *First Explorations of Kentucky* (Louisville, Ky.: Morton, 1898), 170; Cooper, "Notices of Big-Bone Lick," 214–15.

13. William Cooper, J. A. Smith, and James E. Dekay, "Report of Messrs. Cooper, J. A. Smith, and Dekay, to the Lyceum of Natural History, on a Collection of Fossil Bones, Disinterred at Big Bone Lick, Kentucky, in September, 1830, and Recently Brought to This City, (New York)," *Monthly American Journal of Geology and Natural Science* 1 (1831): 43–44; Cooper, "Notices of Big-Bone Lick," 172, 174, 206.

14. Cooper, Smith, and Dekay, "Report to the Lyceum," 44; Richard Owen, "Fossil Mammalia," in Charles Darwin, *The Zoology of the Voyage of H.M.S.* Beagle (London: Smith, Elder, 1840), 1:68–72; Richard Harlan, "Description of the Jaws, Teeth, and Clavicle of the *Megalonyx laqueatus*," *Monthly American Journal of Geology and Natural Science* 1 (1831): 75–76.

15. Kurtén and Anderson, *Pleistocene Mammals*, 143–44; Elaine Anderson, "Who's Who in the Pleistocene: A Mammalian Bestiary," in *Quaternary Extinctions*, ed. Paul S. Martin and Richard G. Klein (Tucson: University of Arizona Press, 1984), 54; Lange, *Ice Age Mammals*, 89.

16. Cooper, "Notices of Big-Bone Lick," 172, 213, 214.

17. Ibid., 214, 210–11.

18. Ibid., 213, 215, 217; Thomas D. Matijasic, "Science, Religion, and the Fossils at Big Bone Lick," *Journal of the History of Biology* 20, no. 3 (1987): 420.

19. Cooper, "Notices of Big-Bone Lick," 211–12.

20. Maximilian, Prince of Wied, *Travels in the Interior of North America*, in Thwaites, *Early Western Travels*, 12:156; Anonymous [Gazley], "Notice of the Osseous Remains," 141.

11. Other Mammoth Changes

1. Charles Lyell, *Travels in North America* (New York: Wiley and Putnam, 1845), 2:53, 59.

2. Ibid., 55; Amos Butler, "Observations on Faunal Changes," *Bulletin of the Brookville Society of Natural History* 1 (1885): 8.

3. Lyell, *Travels*, 2:55–56.

4. Ibid., 56–58.

5. Charles Lyell, "On the Geological Position of the *Mastodon giganteum* and Associated Fossil Remains at Bigbone Lick, Kentucky, and Other Localities in the United States and Canada," *American Journal of Science and Arts* 46 (1844): 320–23.

6. Loren Eiseley, *Darwin's Century* (Garden City, N.Y.: Anchor Books, 1961), 67, 112.

7. John C. Greene, *The Death of Adam* (Ames: Iowa State University Press, 1959), 155–66.

8. Charles Darwin, *On the Origin of Species, A Facsimile of the First Edition with an Introduction by Ernst Mayr* (Cambridge, Mass.: Harvard University Press, 1964), viii, xii–xiii, xvi–xvii.

9. David Young, *The Discovery of Evolution* (London: Cambridge University Press, 1992), 138; William H. Hobbs, "Nathaniel Southgate Shaler," *Transactions of the Wisconsin Academy of Sciences, Arts, and Letters* 15 (1904–1907): 927; Nathaniel S. Shaler, "On the Age of the Bison in the Ohio Valley," in Joel A. Allen, "The American Bisons, Living and Extinct," *Memoirs of the Museum of Comparative Zoology* 4, no. 10 (1876): 236; Nathaniel S. Shaler, "Notes on the Investigations of the Kentucky Survey," in *Kentucky Geological Survey Reports of Progress*, n.s., 3 (1877): 69; Willard R. Jillson, *Big Bone Lick* (Louisville, Ky.: Standard Printing, 1936), 62, 68–69.

10. Shaler, "Notes on Investigations," 69; Jillson, *Big Bone Lick*, 68–69; Allen, "The American Bisons," 32–33; William D. Funkhouser, *Wild Life in Kentucky* (Frankfort: Kentucky Geological Survey, 1925), 31; William D. Funkhouser and William S. Webb, *Ancient Life in Kentucky* (Frankfort: Kentucky Geological Survey, 1928), 43; Arthur C. McFarlan, *Geology of Kentucky* (Lexington: University of Kentucky, 1943), 245.

11. Shaler, "Notes on Investigations," 67.

12. Shaler, "On the Age of the Bison," 233.

13. Ibid., 234; Shaler, "Notes on Investigations," 68.

14. Shaler, "Notes on Investigations," 68–69; Shaler, "On the Age of the Bison," 234.

15. Shaler, "Notes on Investigations," 70; Nathaniel S. Shaler,

"Note on the Occurrence of the Remains of *Tarandus rangifer* Gray, at Big Bone Lick in Kentucky," *Proceedings of the Boston Society of Natural History* 13 (1869–1871): 167.

16. Hobbs, "Nathaniel Southgate Shaler," 924–25; Nathaniel S. Shaler, *The Autobiography of Nathaniel Southgate Shaler with a Supplementary Memoir by His Wife* (Boston: Houghton Mifflin, 1909), 247–48.

17. Christopher C. Graham, "The Mammoths' Graveyard," *Boone County Recorder*, February 22, 1877; Kenneth B. Tankersley, "The Potential for Early-Man Sites at Big Bone Lick, Kentucky," *Tennessee Anthropologist* 10, no. 1 (1985): 28; Reuben G. Thwaites, *Afloat on the Ohio* (Chicago: Way and Williams, 1897), 198.

18. John U. Lloyd, "When Did the American Mammoth and Mastodon Become Extinct?" *Records of the Past* 3, pt. 1 (1904): 44.

19. Oliver P. Hay, *The Pleistocene of North America and Its Vertebrated Animals from the States East of the Mississippi River and from the Canadian Provinces East of Longitude 95°* (Washington, D.C.: Carnegie Institution of Washington, 1923), 146, 160–61.

20. Björn Kurtén and Elaine Anderson, *Pleistocene Mammals of North America* (New York: Columbia University Press, 1980), 351–52; Kenneth B. Tankersley, "Ice Age Giants of the Ohio Valley and Lower Great Lakes Region," in Bradley T. Lepper, *Ohio Archaeology* (Wilmington, Ohio: Orange Frazer, 2005), 37.

21. Kurtén and Anderson, *Pleistocene Mammals*, 344–45, 351–54; Elaine Anderson, "Who's Who in the Pleistocene: A Mammalian Bestiary," in *Quaternary Extinctions*, ed. Paul S. Martin and Richard G. Klein (Tucson: University of Arizona Press, 1984), 83, 86; Ian M. Lange, *Ice Age Mammals of North America* (Missoula, Mont.: Mountain Press, 2002), 166–68, 172–74, 176–78; Jeffrey J. Saunders, "North American Mammutidae," in Jeheskel Shoshani and Pascal Tassy, *The Proboscidea* (Oxford: Oxford University Press, 1996), 274–75.

22. Jillson, *Big Bone Lick*, 68–70; Willard R. Jillson, *The Extinct Vertebrata of the Pleistocene in Kentucky* (Frankfort, Ky.: Roberts Printing, 1968), 39; Funkhouser and Webb, *Ancient Life*, 42; Allen, "The American Bisons," 22; Joseph Leidy, "In the Museum of Comparative Zoology at Harvard College," *Proceedings of the Academy of Natural Sciences of Philadelphia* 22 (1870): 97; Funkhouser, *Wild Life*, 31.

23. Kurtén and Anderson, *Pleistocene Mammals*, 299–300; Anderson, "Who's Who," 69; Lange, *Ice Age Mammals*, 161.

24. Ray Tanner and Dennis Vesper, "A Fossil Bone Collection from Big Bone Lick, Kentucky," *Ohio Archaeologist* 31, no. 4 (1981): 11–13.

25. "Geological Treasury Unearthed," *Enquirer (Covington)*, August 20, 1960; Edwin W. Teale, *Wandering through Winter* (New York: Dodd, Mead, 1966), 245, 248.

12. Agents of Extinction

1. C. Bertrand Schultz, Lloyd G. Tanner, Frank C. Whitmore Jr., Louis L. Ray, and Ellis C. Crawford, "Paleontologic Investigations at Big Bone Lick State Park, Kentucky: A Preliminary Report," *Science* 142 (1963): 1168; Schultz et al., "Big Bone Lick, Kentucky," *Museum Notes, University of Nebraska State Museum* 33 (1967): 4–5; William H. Lowthert IV, "Resource Use and Settlement Patterning around the Saline Springs and Salt Licks in Big Bone Lick State Park, Boone County, Kentucky" (master's thesis, University of Kentucky, 1998), 48.

2. James H. Gunnerson, University of Nebraska State Museum, Lincoln, personal correspondence, August 20, 1974; Kenneth B. Tankersley, "The Potential for Early-Man Sites at Big Bone Lick, Kentucky," *Tennessee Anthropologist* 10, no. 1 (1985): 38–46.

3. Schultz et al., "Paleontologic Investigations," 1168–69; Schultz et al., "Big Bone Lick," 6; C. Bertrand Schultz, Frank C. Whitmore Jr., and Lloyd G. Tanner, "Pleistocene Mammals and Stratigraphy of Big Bone Lick State Park, Kentucky [abstract]," *Geological Society of America Special Paper 87* (1966), 262–63; Louis L. Ray, "Geomorphology and Quaternary Geology of the Glaciated Ohio River Valley—A Reconnaissance Study," *Geological Survey Professional Paper 826* (1974), 70.

4. Tankersley, "Potential for Early-Man Sites at Big Bone Lick," 38, 41.

5. Betsy Levin, Patricia C. Ives, Charles L. Oman, and Meyer Rubin, "U.S. Geological Survey Radiocarbon Dates VIII," *Radiocarbon* 7 (1965): 374; Patricia C. Ives, Betsy Levin, Charles L. Oman, and Meyer Rubin, "U.S. Geological Survey Radiocarbon Dates IX," *Radiocarbon* 9 (1967): 507.

6. Schultz et al., "Paleontologic Investigations," 1168; Schultz et al., "Big Bone Lick," 4–5.

7. Schultz et al., "Paleonotologic Investigations," 1168; Schultz et al., "Big Bone Lick," 5; Meyer Rubin and Sarah M. Berthold, "U.S. Geological Survey Radiocarbon Dates VI," *Radiocarbon* 3 (1961): 88; Levin et al., "Radiocarbon Dates VIII," 374.

8. Schultz et al., "Paleontologic Investigations," 1168; Schultz et al., "Big Bone Lick," 5–6; John A. Rowe, "Fossil Horses from Big Bone Lick, Kentucky [abstract]," *Ohio Journal of Science* 82, no. 2 (1982): 26.

9. Schultz et al., "Paleontologic Investigations," 1168–69; Schultz et al., "Big Bone Lick," 5–6; Tankersley, "Potential for Early-Man Sites at Big Bone Lick," 41.

10. Schultz et al., "Big Bone Lick," 6.

11. Kenneth B. Tankersley, "Bison Exploitation by Late Fort Ancient Peoples in the Central Ohio River Valley," *North American Archaeologist* 7, no. 4 (1986): 295–96, 301; Tankersley, "Potential for Early-Man Sites at Big Bone Lick," 29–30; Lowthert, "Resource Use," 61, 153.

12. Stanley E. Hedeen, *Natural History of the Cincinnati Region* (Cincinnati: Cincinnati Museum Center, 2006), 45, 65, 67.

13. Björn Kurtén and Elaine Anderson, *Pleistocene Mammals of North America* (New York: Columbia University Press, 1980), 301, 317, 362.

14. Thomas V. Lowell, Kevin M. Savage, C. Scott Brockman, and Robert Stuckenrath, "Radiocarbon Analyses from Cincinnati, Ohio, and Their Implications for Glacial Stratigraphic Interpretations," *Quaternary Research* 34 (1990): 1–10.

15. Hazel R. Delcourt, Paul A. Delcourt, Gary R. Wilkins, and E. Newman Smith Jr., "Vegetational History of the Cedar Glades Regions of Tennessee, Kentucky, and Missouri during the Past 30,000 Years," *ASB [Association of Southeastern Biologists] Bulletin* 33, no. 4 (1986): 133–34.

16. Ives et al., "Radiocarbon Dates IX," 507.

17. Delcourt et al., "Vegetational History," 133–34; David G. Anderson, Lisa D. O'Steen, and Kenneth E. Sassaman, "Environmental and Chronological Considerations," in David G. Anderson and Kenneth E. Sassaman, *The Paleoindian and Early Archaic Southeast* (Tuscaloosa: University of Alabama Press, 1996), 3–5; Hedeen, *Natural History*, 25.

18. Daniel C. Fisher, "Extinctions of Proboscideans in North America," in Jeheskel Shoshani and Pascal Tassy, *The Proboscidea* (Oxford: Oxford University Press, 1996), 298.

19. Ian M. Lange, *Ice Age Mammals of North America* (Missoula, Mont.: Mountain Press, 2002), 188–89.

20. Tankersley, "Potential for Early-Man Sites at Big Bone Lick," 33; Fisher, "Extinctions of Proboscideans," 299.

21. Shepard Krech III, *The Ecological Indian* (New York: Norton, 1999), 41–42.

22. Zadok Cramer, *The Navigator*, 8th ed. (Pittsburgh: Cramer, Spear, and Eichbaum, 1814), in *Who's Who on the Ohio River and Its Tributaries*, ed. Ethel C. Leahy (Cincinnati: E. C. Leahy, 1931), 157; letter from William Clark to Thomas Jefferson, November 10, 1807, in Howard C. Rice Jr., "Jefferson's Gift of Fossils to the Museum of Natural History in Paris," *Proceedings of the American Philosophical Society* 95, no. 6 (1951): 602; Alexander Wilson, *Wilson's American Ornithology* (Boston: Otis, Broaders, 1840), 246–53.

23. Hedeen, *Natural History*, 66–69.

24. Ibid., 67, 69; Lange, *Ice Age Mammals*, 196.

25. Richard A. Kerr, "Three Degrees of Consensus," *Science* 305 (2004): 932–34; Robert H. Socolow, "Can We Bury Global Warming?" *Scientific American* 293 (2005): 49–55; Dan Hassert, "Project Traps Carbon Dioxide," *Kentucky Post (Covington)*, August 8, 2006.

Index